COMPASSION
VERSUS
GUILT
and other essays

COMPASSION
VERSUS
GUILT
and other essays

Thomas Sowell

William Morrow and Company, Inc.
New York

Library of Congress Cataloging-in-Publication Data

Sowell, Thomas, 1930–
    Compassion versus guilt and other essays.
    Collection of newspaper articles.
    Includes index.
    1. United States—Politics and government—1981–
2. United States—Social policy—1980–
3. United States—Economic policy—1981–
4. United States—Race relations. 5. Afro-Americans—
Social conditions—1975–   . 6. Afro-Americans—
Economic conditions. I. Title.
E876.S59   1987   973.927   87-7906
ISBN 0-688-07114-7

Printed in the United States of America

First Edition

1 2 3 4 5 6 7 8 9 10

BOOK DESIGN BY KAREN BATTEN

To Agnes

Contents

Introduction

These are essays of the 1980s—the decade which has seen attempts to change political direction in America, in the most fundamental way since the New Deal. The resulting political clashes have gone deeper than usual, emotionally as well as intellectually, and ultimately involve differences in our whole vision of man. These commentaries on the issues of the 1980s therefore span a wide range of enduring concerns.

At the center of many controversies is the role of compassion. Guilt is often confused with compassion—to the detriment of the whole society, and to the special detriment of the least fortunate members of society. The first essay seeks to clarify this crucial distinction. Its theme underlies much of the later discussions of specific issues such as education, crime, foreign aid, or affirmative action.

Another political concept often heard in our times is "solution." Early in these essays, I argue that there are no real solutions in politics—only trade-offs. That theme also recurs in the essays that follow, and extends to foreign policy as well as domestic issues, to economics as well as law, to educational issues no less than to issues of race and sex.

All these essays were first published in newspapers. The trade-offs that this involved seem to me to have more pluses than minuses. The newspaper format imposes limitations of space and approach, but writing for the general public also gives a freedom not always possible when writing for a more academic audience. The public at large seldom has as much dogmatism as intellectuals, and is less preoccupied with putting labels on things, or consumed with its own cleverness. It is therefore easier to write straight to the point for such an audience, without having to surround every statement with fortifications against distortion, misrepresentation, pigeon-holing, or the thousand other games that intellectuals play. In short, these essays were written for people with common sense—a rare commodity among those who consider themselves deep thinkers.

Most of these essays were first published as op-ed columns in newspapers around the country via the Scripps-Howard News Service. Some, however, were written for specific newspapers. "The U.N. Promotes War—Not Peace" was written for the *Los Angeles Times,* as was "Social Security: A Fraudulent Pyramid Scheme." "Authorized Lying" was written for the *Washington Times* and "Reagan's Economic Policies" for the *Washington Post.* "Mathematically Eliminated" was written for the *Wall Street Journal.* All others were published through the Scripps-Howard News Service. The kind permission of all the above has made this book possible.

—THOMAS SOWELL

Hoover Institution
Stanford, California   94305

I

SOCIAL POLICY

Compassion versus Guilt

Many years ago, in a Third World country, I noticed by the side of the road a ragged and forlorn little boy, who bore an uncanny resemblance to my son. It was a momentary but penetrating shock—followed by a sober realization that that was what my son might be like, if we had been born there instead of in the United States.

"There, but for the grace of God, go I." There are many occasions to say that—whether looking at the poor, the ill, the criminal, or the victims of tyranny. Even the most ardent believer in individual merit must recognize that where you happen to have been born, how you were raised, or where you happen to have been located when opportunity or disaster came along, can make all the difference in the world.

Much of what has been done, or attempted, for the benefit of the unfortunates of this nation or the world, reflects in part a humbling understanding that our personal good fortune may not all be as richly deserved as we might like to think. While this feeling is both sensible and humane, the policies that follow from it are not always wise or effective. Sometimes they are catastrophic.

While the fate of an individual may contain a large element of luck, the fates of whole peoples and civilizations reflect much more. Effects have causes. Many of the great epidemics of history were not unrelated to filth. It is no accident that cholera died out as sanitation improved, and persists today in countries where filth is a way of life.

It is no accident that the Japanese have prospered in their own land, though it is almost devoid of natural resources. They have also prospered in the Western Hemisphere, from Canada to Brazil, in the face of racism, discrimination, and wartime internment by a number of countries. The Japanese in Brazil now own almost three-quarters as much land as there is in Japan. Ask the Chrysler Corporation if the Japanese are efficient.

Peoples are different, and these differences have consequences. Much of our fashionable deep thinking on social issues—in the media and academia alike—consists of elaborate denials or evasions of this basic reality.

Many of our attempts to share our good fortune with others, at home and abroad, have undermined the very efforts, standards and values that make that good fortune possible. Trying to ease our own guilt feelings is very different from trying to advance those less fortunate.

For the individual, it may be a windfall gain that he was born into circumstances that made it possible—perhaps easy—for him to meet high educational or other standards, and thereby advance to prosperity. But lowering the standards for those unable to meet them only endangers the very benefits these standards produce. Standards do not exist for no reason.

We are not just being fussy when we expect a medical student to have mastered much complex knowledge before he becomes a doctor. If his background did not prepare him to master such difficulties, then his misfortune should not be multiplied as the misfortunes of his patients.

Mathematics and physics are not mere hurdles placed capriciously in the path of aspiring engineers. You don't want to drive across an engineer's bridge, unless he knows how to make sure it can take the weight and stress.

Punctuality is not just a fetish, for people whose work in a factory or office has to be coordinated with others. It is not just cultural imperialism to tell someone to turn off his blaring radio, on a job where people have to be able to hear themselves think.

To ignore standards is not to share benefits, but to destroy benefits.

Whether in a secular or a religious sense, it is right to say: "There, but for the grace of God, go I." But the corollary is not to destroy the grace of God, in the name of equality.

No doubt many a mugger or murderer would have taken a different path in life if his home or community had given him different values—or perhaps, any values. But to ease the standards and turn him loose helps nobody. Neither does reciting the magic word, "rehabilitation."

Deep thinkers who look everywhere for the mysterious causes of poverty, ignorance, crime, and war need look no further than their own mirrors. We are all born into this world poor and ignorant, and with thoroughly selfish and barbaric impulses. Those of us who turn out any other way do so largely through the efforts of others, who civilized us before we got big enough to do too much damage to the world or ourselves. But for these efforts, we might well be on welfare or in the penitentiary.

We owe gratitude for those efforts, not guilt for those who didn't get them. We certainly cannot make it up to those without values by easing standards and letting them become a burden and a threat to others. That is buying a good conscience or a good image with an I.O.U. to be paid by somebody else.

Those who want to share their good fortune can share the sources of that good fortune—the skills, values, and discipline that mean productivity. Those who want to ease their burden of guilt should seek professional help, at their own expense—not make policy at everyone else's expense.

—February 26, 1984

The High Cost of Hoodlums

Hoodlums are not simply a nuisance or a danger. They are an expensive luxury. Most poor people would just as soon do without them, but they don't have that choice.

Prices in low-income neighborhoods are often higher than prices for the same goods in middle-class neighborhoods. Sometimes the quality is lower as well. Customers may also be treated with less courtesy, consideration or efficiency. All this is part of the price of living in a neighborhood where crime, violence, and vandalism are more prevalent.

When academic researchers discovered that "the poor pay more," their first reaction was that it showed the evils of American society. But, despite the popularity of such conclusions among intellectuals and the media, there are serious economic reasons why hoodlumism raises prices and lowers quality.

The direct costs of a higher rate of vandalism, shoplifting, and hold-ups are obvious. The honest customers pay these costs in higher prices. Even in a high-crime neighborhood, most people may be law-abiding, but they still end up paying for those among them who are not.

They pay indirectly as well. Some stores close up and move out when the strain of coping with violence, vandalism, and harassment becomes too much. Once the store is gone, the costs of hoodlumism no longer show up in its prices. But these costs may now be even greater, in terms of having to travel longer distances to find a store, a pharmacy, or a place to eat. For those too poor to afford an automobile, this "price" may be very high, especially if they are elderly, ill, or a woman alone.

The price indexes that statisticians put together do not include the costs of an elderly or sick person's having to wait on the corner in the winter for a bus to go to the nearest market, or the cost of a mother's having to walk for blocks at night through a high-crime neighborhood, looking for a drug store for medicine for a sick child. But the increased scarcity of stores is a very real cost imposed on the poor by hoodlumism.

Precautions taken by stores that remain also raise costs. In some neighborhoods, heavy grates have to be put in front of a store when it closes at night, to avoid break-ins. Guards patrol the aisles during the day. In short, extra costs are added 24 hours a day.

More subtle costs are also added. Store space is used differently in low-crime and high-crime neighborhoods. Markets in high-crime neighborhoods must be careful not to have merchandise displayed right inside the entrance, where someone can grab it and run. In neighborhoods where crime and vandalism are not such preoccupations, virtually every square foot of store space can be used to display merchandise and earn money. Low-value items may even be set outside the store, with no one watching them. Pay telephones and newspaper dispensing machines can be installed outside, to earn more money, without worrying that they will be broken into or put out of commission by vandals.

When the same sized store has very different amounts of space available for making money in different neighborhoods, then the prices charged are also going to be different. When it has to pay very different insurance rates for fire or other destruction, those differences are also reflected in the prices.

Stores that sell appliances or other items on credit charge prices that vary with the risk of default. In neighborhoods where the risk of default is very high, the honest once more pay for the dishonest. The same principle applies when some tenants don't pay their rent.

When a neighborhood is an undesirable place to work, you are not going to get the most desirable people to work there, either as clerks or managers. Good people are always in demand, and they can pick and choose their location. The net result is that high-crime areas are likely to get less efficient managers and less-courteous clerks—charging higher prices.

Being poor is expensive. Statistics on poverty are too optimistic, to the extent that they ignore the higher costs of living in low-income neighborhoods that are also high-crime neighborhoods.

None of this is difficult to understand as economics. What is difficult is to get the political and judicial systems to face this reality.

Politicians who represent slums or ghettoes are not going to get cheers or votes by saying that the basic problems of these communities are in the communities themselves. In politics, whatever the issue, someone else is always to blame. In this case, "greedy" merchants and landlords are blamed. And when these "greedy" merchants and landlords pull out of neighborhoods they are supposed to be exploiting, then they are blamed for that too.

The eagerness of intellectuals and the media to see American society as rotten lends weight to these political visions. If it was only a question of pinning blame on someone, then merchants, landlords and bankers could be left to either defend themselves or ignore the rhetoric. (Probably the latter.) But when very serious problems facing the poor are mistakenly diagnosed, the cures prescribed can make their situation worse.

When judges delay the eviction of tenants who do not pay their rent, they increase the costs to tenants who do pay their rent. They also make housing a less attractive investment. It is not uncommon for a city with an acute housing shortage to have plenty of vacant office space.

Judges are not "compassionate" to office renters. Political crusaders seldom pass rent control laws for offices.

When politicians and community activists in low-income neighborhoods pressure merchants to hire people they don't want, or to contribute to miscellaneous community "causes," the net economic effect is to add to the already high costs of doing business there. In the short run, it is possible to get away with milking businessmen who are there. But in the long run no one should be surprised to find them leaving—and few replacements coming in.

These kinds of political approaches do not merely happen to be counterproductive. They are necessarily counterproductive. Hoodlums create very real costs. If you are serious, that means lowering those costs, not trying to put them on somebody else.

Judges, social workers, and politicians who want to give hoodlums "another chance" for "rehabilitation" need to think about giving the people another chance instead, by cracking down on hoodlumism. The poor need it more than anyone else.

—January 27, 1984

The Wonderful World of "Solutions"

There was once a fine television program for children called "The Wonderful World of Disney." Many deep thinkers and social moralizers have their own adult counterpart—the wonderful world of "solutions."

The tragedies inherent in the human condition are seen

by them as "problems" to which there are "solutions." Trade-offs are not good enough for the morally anointed. There must be solutions.

Safety is an example. According to solution-seekers, heart transplants should not be done unless they are "safe." New medicines should not be introduced until they are safe. Nuclear power plants should not be built until they are safe.

People are dying from all this safety.

Life-saving drugs are being kept out of the United States by laws that require years of delay to meet incredible safety requirements—even for drugs already widely used in Europe. People die while waiting.

Most patients are at death's door before they are ready to try anything as desperate as a heart transplant. But surgeons should say "no" to them until it is safe, if we are to believe the solution-seekers.

Nuclear power plants have a long, worldwide record of safety vastly exceeding that in coal mining, oil drilling, or other ways of producing energy. The annual toll of deaths among coal miners, oil workers, lumberjacks, and others is a sobering reminder of the tragic price paid for our heat, light, and transportation.

The less nuclear power, the more people die producing the same energy in more dangerous ways.

Yet none of these painful trade-offs enter the wonderful world of solutions.

Even policemen who have a split second to make a decision, on which their own life or death can depend, are supposed to produce solutions. Armed criminals are to be put safely behind bars through methods that harm no one.

Just what these methods are has not yet been revealed, but vehement solution-seekers are convinced that "training" in these methods offers a solution.

In the wonderful world of solutions, someone is always

to blame when things go wrong. Our courts are clogged with lawsuits from this principle.

If children die from a vaccine, big damages must be imposed on the company that produced it. It doesn't matter if no vaccine can possibly be 100 percent safe, or if the number of children who die without the vaccine is many times greater. There has just got to be a solution. (One drug company's solution has been to stop selling vaccine.)

None of this matters to zealous "consumer advocates" who crusade against anything with bad side effects. But practically everything in the world has some bad side effects, including consumer advocates.

Much of the furor over the Reagan Administration's policies toward South Africa assumes that there is some "solution" which Americans can impose from 8,000 miles away.

But neither American rhetoric nor an American boycott is going to change South Africa's racial policy.

A boycott of South Africa would have two results. First, it would give boycotters a good feeling and good publicity. It would also cost blacks in South Africa their jobs in American firms, which are usually some of the best jobs available to them.

In other words, American protesters would be better off and South African blacks worse off. This is hardly a solution. It isn't even a decent trade-off.

I must confess to a certain envy of those who live in the wonderful world of solutions. Life's painful trade-offs, which plague the rest of us, leave them in untroubled bliss and moral certainty.

Even when their demands are not met, they can vent their frustration by blaming it on the bad guys. It is never necessary for them to reconsider whether the real world corresponds to their vision, or to limit their choices to the alternatives actually available.

Some solution-seekers may admit that they don't have a

real alternative available yet, but think that pressing for the best will at least make things better.

But that's not the way it has worked in history. Those who found the authoritarianism of the Shah of Iran intolerable did not make things better by undermining him and setting the stage for the Ayatollahs.

Bringing down the chaotic Weimar republic meant unleashing Hitler. The autocratic Czar of Russia now seems almost quaint by comparison with the Communist tyranny that succeeded him.

Making hard choices among the alternatives actually available means accepting the trade-offs that still leave much evil in the world. But crusades in the wonderful world of solutions turn many unhappy situations into utter catastrophes.

—March 1, 1985

Child Abuse

Child abuse is one of the most despicable of all crimes. But if anything can make it worse, it is having it become a fad issue among deep thinkers.

Many tragedies revolve around child abuse—tragedies in the very real sense of agonizing situations with no real "solution," but only trade-offs that can salvage something from the wreckage. If authorities don't act quickly and decisively, there can be irreparable damage. But if they act too hastily, without really knowing what is going on, they can disrupt innocent families, smear the reputations of decent individuals, or needlessly destroy the trust on which the child's own well-being depends.

Deep thinkers aren't into tragedies and trade-offs. Deep thinkers are going to find "solutions"—whether they exist or not.

Even when the child has clearly been abused—bruises, broken bones, cigarette burns, etc.—deep thinkers have a "solution": Put the parents in therapy. This is a faith which passeth all understanding. There is no hard evidence that it works. Meanwhile, children and infants are put back into the hands of rotten people who belong in jail. Some children have been killed after being put back with abusive parents.

California is one of the states mesmerized by rhetoric into letting people off the hook after they have done horrible and disgusting things to small children and even babies. Through the magic of psychotherapy and social workers visiting the house occasionally, families are "kept together." How does the reality compare with the rhetoric?

As so often happens, one of the leading exponents of this experimental program has been given the job of evaluating whether it is a success. After more than a million dollars worth of research money was spent, Professor Michael Wald of the Stanford Law School produced his report. The bottom line was: We don't know.

Professor Wald was more honest than many others in a similar position. He said that the research "raises some questions about the desirability of the current approach." Too late now, Mike. The experimental program, which began in little San Mateo county, has spread like wildfire across the state of California. It has been made a model for federal legislation.

When a political crusade is on, there is no time to wait and see if anybody knows what they are talking about.

At the other extreme, when there is only a suspicion of child abuse, without any real evidence, there is the same headlong rush to judgment—and "solutions." Deep thinkers have set up the dogma that little children don't lie about such things. In one case, however, the child not only lied but faked the evidence—which chemical analysis showed to be ink from a red marking pen instead of blood.

Parents in bitter divorce cases have been known to accuse each other of child abuse—and to either pressure or mislead the child into false statements damaging to the other parent. But the biggest tragedy comes when politics hypes the pressure for authorities to find child abuse, and puts big bucks in the hands of the social work establishment for dealing with it.

Once the authorities get your child in their clutches—however flimsy the reason—they've got you in their clutches. You've got to play along with the therapy if you want to have your own flesh and blood back in your home again. You may be pressured to "admit" things that never happened, just so the authorities' records look good.

How flimsy can the evidence be? One Colorado couple had their daughter held for months because she was so unusually small for her age that neglect was suspected. Both her mother and her grandfather were less than five feet tall when fully grown.

In a Minnesota case, a couple lost custody of their children for several months on the testimony of a man arrested for child molestation. He had made a deal with the prosecutor to implicate others. The fact that such deals have been a great source of perjury down through history apparently did not bother the prosecutor. Neither did the children's steadfast denials, nor a doctor's report which failed to corroborate the charges. Nor did the accuser's public retraction of the charges.

The problem is that, once the authorities get into one of these cases, they cannot simply admit that they were wrong and back off. That would open them up to lawsuits and political backlash.

The bigger problems, which reaches well beyond child

abuse, is that we are too easily stampeded by loud, self-righteous groups with a vested interest in both problems and "solutions." Many of the estimates so gullibly trumpeted as statistical facts by the media originate in such groups.

—April 7, 1986

The Green Bigots

The wilderness recreation lobby is called many things, but the best name I have heard for them is "the green bigots." Bigots think that their way is the only way, and that other people don't count. This has long been the attitude of those who call themselves "environmentalists."

The green bigots try to give the impression that they are trying to save the last few remaining patches of wilderness, before it disappears under a covering of asphalt and concrete. In reality, the land owned by the National Park Service alone is larger than Great Britain. The land owned by the U.S. Forest Service is larger than France. In addition, the Fish and Wildlife Service owns land that is larger than Holland, Israel, Belgium and Switzerland—combined. Moreover, the federal government has been buying up still more land to add to this in recent years, despite budget deficits and other crying needs.

Many people are unaware of how vast an area has been set aside, at public expense, for outdoor recreational purposes. Nor are they aware of how relentlessly the wilderness recreation lobby has used its political clout to make it more difficult for millions of ordinary citizens to have access to this enormous expanse of land that is supposedly being "preserved" for "the people."

Tourist facilities are being torn down. Access by automobile and bus is being blocked. Powered tourist boats and rafts are scheduled to be banned from the Colorado River through the Grand Canyon. The point is to give preferential access to those with the lifestyle of the environmentalists and keep out ordinary city people with limited vacation time and kids who cannot be turned loose in the wild. If you don't have the leisure, the money, the physique or the "commitment" to a special lifestyle, then the wilderness recreation lobby doesn't want you allowed in anymore. All their talk about "the people" is political rhetoric. If you can't afford to have your family learn mountaineering, horseback riding, skiing, camping, or the mysteries of white water canoeing, you are going to have less and less access to more and more public land.

The perpetuation of such special privileges for the environmentalists into the indefinite future is referred to politically as concern for "posterity." That is, the posterity of the environmentalists is to continue to enjoy the same advantages over the posterity of the rest of the society— which is to continue to pay, and continue to find obstacles put in their way when they want to see what they have paid for.

What society pays for the recreational privileges that a small and affluent group of Sierra Clubbers and other environmental extremists want limited to themselves is not simply the money to maintain and acquire public land. Nation-sized expanses of land contain vast amounts of resources that could mean many jobs, much housing, and an improved standard of living for many Americans. The issue is not whether there should be any recreational wilderness, but whether there should be some sense of balance between the wilderness recreation lobby—the green bigots—and the large majority of Americans.

Under pressure from these lobbyists, the Environmental Protection Agency recently proposed a plan to save fish from "acid rain." The cost worked out to about $16,000 per fish. It was typical of the heedless zeal of environmentalism.

Like other special interest groups, the wilderness recreationists try to represent their own particular benefits as *national* benefits—and to ignore the costs to others. Their "party line" is preached as the only truth, not only to tourists but in a constant din in the media. It is virtually impossible to watch a television nature program without getting a political speech about how government ought to preserve land from encroachment by "man" (said with just the right amount of distaste).

Some of the green bigots are now resorting to sabotage against industries operating in the wilderness, such as loggers and oil companies. They even have a book on how to sabotage those who dare to think that they have the same rights as the self-anointed environmentalists.

What environmentalism illustrates, to a frightening ex tent, is how vulnerable this democracy has become to the rhetoric of small groups made shrill by self-righteousness. Their political success reveals how unthinkingly we have become conditioned to respond on cue to certain pious words, much like the conditioned reflexes of Pavlov's dog.

—January 17, 1986

Envy and "Social Justice"

Envy used to be one of the seven deadly sins. But now it is the prime political virtue, under its new name—"social justice."

The fact that some groups are poor because of historic injustices done to them has been taken by many as a blank check to consider all lower income groups victims of injustice. In many parts of the world, however, those initially in dire poverty have, over the generations, raised themselves to an above-average level of prosperity, by great effort and painful sacrifice. Now the deep thinkers come along and want to redistribute what they earned to others who were initially more fortunate but less hard-working.

In a number of Third World countries, the indigenous peoples refused to do the gruelling, and sometimes dangerous, work of building railroads, mining, or working on rubber, tea, or sugar plantations—usually because they had ample fertile land of their own from which to make a living, and thus had no need to subject themselves to such ordeals. Less fortunate people, such as coolies from China or India, were brought in to do the work that the natives spurned. This happened from colonial Malaya and Ceylon to Peru, Fiji, Kenya and Uganda, among other places.

These Chinese and Indians, used to eking out a hard existence in their homelands, often responded to their new opportunities by saving money out of what looked like mere "subsistence" wages to others, later becoming peddlers, tiny shopkeepers, or farmers on small patches of land.

The first step upward often involved still more long and unrelenting work, with little to show for it at the beginning. The Chinese shopkeepers in Southeast Asia were notorious for their long hours. A Chinese woman could often be seen working in the fields, in water up to her knees, carrying a baby strapped to her back all the while. The small Indian truck farmers in South Africa could be seen weeding their plots of land by moonlight, after working all day farming and selling the produce door to door. Similar stories could be told of these groups in countries around the world, as well as of the Lebanese in West Africa, and at one time the Jews in a number of countries in Europe, the Middle East or the Western Hemisphere.

Eventually—sometimes only in the second generation—such groups began to rise to prosperity. Their businesses expanded and some of their children became educated professionals. It is then that they are resented and envied by the indigenous peoples. Long after it has been forgotten that the first cotton gins or rice mills were built by the Indians or Chinese, politicians and intellectuals denounce the fact that these groups have "seized control" of the country's cotton gins, rice mills, or other capital assets, using them to "exploit" the people. The fact that many products and services were first brought within the reach of the local populace by these minorities is ignored.

Not only the locals talk like this. Deep thinkers in far off American universities write solemnly about the income "inequities" in Malaysia, where the Chinese make twice as much as the Malays. As consultants, they may even come up with schemes to "correct" such "inequities" in the name of "social justice."

Local politicians go much further. They have even expelled the very groups that have played the key roles in the development of their economy. The 50,000 Indians expelled from Uganda by Idi Amin are the most dramatic recent example, but history is full of similar expulsions of Jews from various countries in Europe and Chinese from countries in Asia.

Even where the more productive groups are not directly expelled, conditions may be made so impossible for them that mass refugee flight results. The classic recent examples of this have been Vietnam's "boat people"—most of whom were Chinese. The Ibos of Nigeria in the 1960s and the Armenians in Turkey during World War I were both massacred in the streets before the survivors were forced to flee.

The time is long overdue to return envy to its former role as one of the seven deadly sins. At the very least, we can stop calling it "social justice."

—October 4, 1985

Withdrawal from Drugs

"If at first you don't succeed, try, try, again—and then give up. Don't be a damn fool about it."

W. C. Fields's wisecrack contained a lot of wisdom. Nowhere does it apply more than in the crusade against drugs.

Drug raids are good politics but they don't make a dent in the problem. The federal government's seizures of cocaine are six times what they were just a few years ago. But the flood of cocaine into the country has continued to be so massive as to drive down the price. A variety of drugs are for sale within a mile of the Drug Enforcement Administration's headquarters in Washington.

The ban on drugs has become Prohibition writ large. Like Prohibition, the ban on drugs has been a financial bonanza for organized crime, and its profits have financed the corruption of law enforcement agencies, politicians, and judges.

Drugs can be hideous things. And those who push drugs are slimy and poisonous. But let us not forget that a similar case was made against alcohol and bootleggers many years ago. Tens of thousands of lives are still lost each year to drunk driving alone. That doesn't count the other lives destroyed or dehumanized under the influence of the bottle.

If drugs and alcohol had never been discovered, this would be a lot better world. But it is a dangerous illusion that we have the omnipotence to undo every evil. The crusading mentality can easily make things worse.

Drugs are inherently a problem for the individual who takes them, but they are a much bigger problem for society—*precisely because they are illegal.* It is their illegality that makes them costly and drives people to desperation to get the money by any means, at anybody else's expense.

The mere cost of production of drugs can be very inexpensive. If an addict could support his addiction for a few dollars a week, he would still be an addict, but he would not have to steal, mug, or kill other people to support his habit. Neither would drug pushers have the financial incentive to try to get children hooked on drugs, if there was no big money in it.

Crusaders cannot accept the fact that they are not God—that they have neither the right nor the competence to run other people's lives. The years that preceded Prohibition saw private citizens take the law into their own hands, entering saloons with axes to destroy bottles of liquor. It was ego-boosting, moral exhibitionism.

When the crusaders finally succeeded in getting the Prohibition amendment added to the U.S. Constitution, it was their crowning triumph—and the nation's tragedy. Organized crime blossomed. So did the corruption of the whole political process.

When national Prohibition ended, many localities passed their own bans on liquor. Bootleggers sometimes financed the campaigns to ban liquor. Their profits depended on liquor's being illegal.

Legalization of narcotics would similarly destroy the profits of today's drug pushers. There is no way that they can compete with drugs that can be mass-produced cheaply by big pharmaceutical companies.

This is not a complete "solution." Nowhere is it written in stone that there are always answers in the back of the book. What we can do as a society is to cut our losses. It is bad enough that some people destroy their own lives with drugs. We don't need to add vast numbers of innocent victims who are robbed, mugged or murdered by addicts trying to get money for a fix.

Like alcohol, drugs can be regulated for content, age required for purchasing, driving under the influence, etc. But this is just one more area where we have to recognize that government has its limits. Ignoring those limits is not only reckless arrogance but dangerous. We finally learned that painful lesson from Prohibition. We need to remember it when it comes to drugs.

—November 29, 1984

Subsidizing Egos

One of the curious features of the modern welfare state is how often its unskilled and so-called "menial" work is done by foreigners. Maids in homes and hotels, agricultural laborers toiling under a hot sun, as well as hospital orderlies, bus boys, sweepers, and other such non-prestigious jobs are often filled disproportionately by aliens.

Despite much fashionable talk which suggests that today jobs are plentiful only for people with hi-tech skills, the cold fact is that thousands of poorly educated Mexicans cross the border every week and go right to work. How can people new to the country and its language constantly keep finding jobs that elude native-born Americans?

Nor is the United States unique. Similar jobs in the Western European welfare states are often filled by people from other parts of the world. They are called "guest workers" and there are literally millions of them.

This pattern tells us something about the welfare state in general. The justification used for taking away what some people have worked for, and giving it to others, is that the recipients are unable to take care of themselves. But if people with even fewer advantages are able to support themselves—and often save money to send home—then it is time to wonder and question.

Some members of society are clearly unable to take care of themselves—the physically or mentally handicapped, for example. But you can see some very healthy-looking people standing in soup lines, and hear middle-class accents among those using food stamps in the stores.

Even worse, many of the deep thinkers in our universities, editorial offices, and social organizations talk as if people are "entitled" to what others have worked for, and should not be forced to take "menial" jobs. It doesn't seem to bother them that others are forced to work to support the idle.

Welfare state spending is sold politically as "compassion" for the unfortunate. But these vast expenditures do not protect people from hunger so much as they protect their egos from having to earn their own food by doing whatever work matches their capabilities.

Studies of multi-problem families show that many of those being supported by the taxpayers are people who didn't bother to learn when they were in school, didn't bother to get work experience or job skills afterwards, and often don't bother to obey the law either. There are consequences to that kind of behavior. What the welfare state does is to force others to pay the consequences.

The alternative is not to leave people to starve. There is far too much work around for anyone to starve. Masses of foreigners who take jobs others won't do prove that. Nor do these jobs leave people at a starvation level. Often the foreigners who take them begin buying a home, opening a little business, or otherwise start moving up after a few tough years. Studies in a number of countries show the average immigrant eventually overtaking the average native-born individual in income. But it takes work and it is no picnic.

The harsh realities of life do not disappear because some people's egos are cushioned by the welfare state. More of the burden is simply carried by others—the decent, working people who pay the taxes and are treated as expendable.

Welfare mothers whose children are in school do not have to be idle—at someone else's expense. As the welfare system is set up, however, a welfare mother would often lose money by taking a job—and might lose other valuable benefits and protections as well. She may not be able to afford the gamble.

The real culprits are those who created a system that makes it dangerous to work and safe to loaf, those who have turned honest work into a shame and made being a parasite respectable.

Such labels as "menial" and "dead-end" jobs disparage the very necessary work of keeping things clean, growing food, or tending children. For young workers especially, the things you can learn on such jobs—responsibility, cooperation, punctuality—can be lifelong assets in many other occupations. Insulating people from such realities is one of many cruelties perpetrated under the banner of "compassion."

—November 1, 1984

Work and Output

When I travel through California's vast agricultural areas, the people I see working in the fields under the hot sun are usually Mexicans. So are many of the people who clean the hotels. But when I have been approached by a panhandler in San Francisco or Los Angeles, it has never been a Mexican.

Almost invariably, the panhandlers have been young, healthy-looking whites with middle-class accents. These men remind me of the old English expression, "sturdy beggars."

One nicely dressed young woman with a well-modulated voice looked so different from the image of a panhandler that I was already past her before I realized that that was what she was. But I have seen her again. She works one of the better business districts of San Francisco.

All I can do is walk past such people. To give them money would be to say that they are somehow better than the Mexicans who have to earn their living by helping to feed the rest of society and by keeping hotels and offices clean. How these young, middle-class people get the *nerve* to ask a black man (whose mother was a maid) for money is beyond me.

What is truly disheartening is what all this means for the future of this country. The whole connection between work and the output we live on is being lost in many people's minds. To many, the country *somehow* has wealth, which we should all share—and "fairly." The most basic fairness of contributing to the efforts that produced what you want to share escapes them completely.

If this confusion were confined to a few parasites, it would be a minor problem. But it has become the hallmark of our deep thinkers on university campuses and in editorial offices. If you want the connection between work and output to disappear, just say the magic word, "compassion."

That works fine on the printed page—which is the ultimate reality for many of the deep thinkers. Meanwhile, back in the real world, the connection between efforts and results remains exactly what it has always been, for society as a whole. What magic words like "compassion" mean is that some must work even harder, so that others don't have to work at all.

Factory workers will have to put in more time on the job, in order that more welfare mothers can sit home and watch soap operas.

The food that is so nobly handed out in soup kitchens or so efficiently "administered" as food stamps was all grown by somebody toiling somewhere. Why should farmers and agricultural laborers be working under a hot sun out in California's valleys, so that others can lounge around the streets of San Francisco or Berkeley and "do their own thing"?

At one time, people who didn't work were called "bums." Today, they have been sanctified as "the homeless."

No doubt there are some tragic cases among those on the street. And no doubt the media will always find them. But, meanwhile, we are raising a whole generation to believe in fairy godmothers. And to vote for them.

A significant part of those who are out on the street today are there because of past theories of our deep thinkers, for whom theories come and go like teenage fads. A portion of the homeless are mentally ill. Some wander the streets, oblivious to traffic, or become prey to the uglier elements of street life. Instead of getting the medication and protection they need in a mental hospital, they are put out on the street because "in the community" became a fad phrase among those who talk about policy, write laws, and strike moral poses.

How long will we continue to let glib talkers lead us around by the nose and use us as guinea pigs for their latest theories?

—September 7, 1984

Chicken Little and Carcinogens

Recently 35 wells were closed down in Silicon Valley because they contained cancer-causing chemicals, presumably as industrial wastes from the computer firms located there. Such actions are often cheered by environmentalists, investigative reporters, "concerned" politicians, and others with a vested interest in moral indignation.

But, before joining this cheering, you should know that the actual amounts of cancer-causing substances in the water from most of the wells that were shut down was less than that in the water from your faucet—and much less than that in colas, wine, or beer.

Professor Bruce Ames, chairman of the biochemistry department at Berkeley, pointed out recently that every meal we eat is full of cancer-causing chemicals—from nature. Professor Ames was not trying to throw a scare into us. On the contrary, he was illustrating the pointlessness of Chicken Little hysteria over often insignificant amounts of man-made carcinogens, compared to vastly more numerous—and sometimes more potent—carcinogens in nature.

The plants we eat as vegetables produce their own toxic pesticides to fight off insects, fungus, and other threats, just as the human body produces chemicals to fight bacteria. According to Professor Ames, "5 basil leaves are 100 times more hazardous than the worst well in Silicon Valley." Altogether, we eat or drink natural pesticides "in amounts at least 10,000 times more than man-made pesticide residues." All this is according to a scientist who has won several prizes in biochemistry.

What are we to do—stop eating? Even that won't do it, because oxygen is also a cancer-causing substance, and so is sunlight. Apparently the only really safe thing to do is to starve in a dungeon while holding your breath.

No one who has lost a loved one to cancer (as I have) can take that horrible disease lightly. But what is both Utopian and hysterical is the impossible dream of getting rid of all man-made dangers—however minute or remote. This has not only exorbitant costs but pathetically little effect.

There has to be some sense of proportion. Cigarette smoking is truly dangerous, and tens of thousands pay for it with their lives each year. Some chemicals are highly toxic, and anyone who dumps them ought to be fined or jailed. But we cannot panic over minute traces of every substance that has harmed laboratory rats when given in astronomical quantities. Moreover, some chemicals that cause cancer in rats do not cause cancer in mice, and vice versa. If there is that much difference between these two closely related species, extrapolating from them to human beings is questionable.

Sometimes panic is not only useless but counterproductive, because many things that are harmful in one way are helpful in another way. Many foods which contain traces of cancer-causing substances also contain cancer-fighting substances. Depending on the proportions, you could be worse off by eliminating such foods from your diet. Cooking meat creates chemicals that can shorten your life, but not cooking it properly—especially if it is pork—can shorten your life a lot faster.

Although people live in many places where the natural radiation from the ground exceeds that from any nuclear power plant, still there is a minute increase in the risk to life from living next to a nuclear facility. But if you decided to move away, driving just 10 miles down the highway would create a risk to your life greater than that of remaining next to the nuclear power plant. People were in fact killed driving away from the Three-Mile Island "disaster," which itself killed nobody.

All life is a matter of proportions and trade-offs. But crusaders don't want to hear about trade-offs. They want "solutions" that produce absolute "safety." Crusaders like to say things like, "We should not sacrifice a single human life to the pursuit of profit."

That's the kind of talk that gets you applause from the environmentalists and a welcome into the ranks of the deep thinkers. But it doesn't save any lives.

The devastating economic impact of environmental hysteria on the nuclear power industry is only a faint foretaste of the massive sacrifices of everyone's standard of living that can be expected if the Chicken Littles get their way. Economic productivity has generated the standard of living which enables us to support a level of health care that has been constantly increasing the human life span. If we let hysteria kill the goose that lays the golden egg, we will be sacrificing our own lives as well.

—March 3, 1986

"Dead-End" Jobs

When was the last time you were in a fast food restaurant, without seeing a "help wanted" sign?

The fast food places I go into, around the country, always seem to be trying to hire somebody. Yet our deep thinkers and moral leaders tell us that people are in soup lines because they just can't find a job.

Working in a fast food restaurant is supposed to be a "dead-end" job. But that's not how the people who work there see it.

A recent study of more than 7,000 people who worked in fast food restaurants showed that most of them saw it as a step toward something better. Most of these people were young (under 20) and worked part-time.

Typically they had worked in fast food places less than two years, so this was not their career. But 90 percent of them said that the job helped them learn how to deal with people and improved their ability to work with others.

Blacks and Hispanics constituted about one-fifth of those fast food employees. These were precisely the people who most felt that the job helped them to become punctual, to improve their grooming, and gave them a sense of the importance of taking care of their money.

Blacks and Hispanics were also more likely than whites to think in terms of wanting to become a manager of a fast food restaurant.

Apparently they don't buy the "dead-end" talk that is so fashionable among intellectuals.

Watching some of the minority youngsters behind the counter at a fast food place near me is an upbeat experience. They are all business. They speak straight English. They are not the kind of wisecracking smart Alecks so popular on television.

42

The great majority of these youngsters will not stay in fast food places the rest of their lives. But what these jobs give them is a foundation of work habits, experience, and references.

In the long run, these are far more important than the paychecks they receive today.

The positive effects of these kinds of jobs are in sharp contrast with the disastrous effects of government job training programs and make-work projects. Youngsters from these programs often fail to get jobs or to hold on to them when they do.

Why the difference?

Government make-work programs are phoney. They teach people to be hustlers, not workers. They accept standards of behavior—and misbehavior—that no employer can accept, if he intends to run his business like a business.

The main thrust of many governmental programs for minorities seems to be to reach the hoodlum, the drug addict, the teenage mother. What happens to the decent people who are struggling to better themselves doesn't seem to matter very much.

We have so overdosed on sociology and media images that it is easy to forget that most people are decent people, even in high-crime neighborhoods. Moreover, these are the kinds of people who are the hope of the future. They are routinely ignored by the government and by deep thinkers.

A couple of years ago, an elderly member of my family passed out on the street in the Bronx. It happened to be a Puerto Rican neighborhood. As she lay there unconscious, her pocket book lying open beside her, people in the neighborhood came to her rescue.

Some directed the traffic around her. Others went to get water. Someone else called an ambulance. Another person held her pocket book and then returned it to her. Not a penny was missing.

Why not build on the decency that is there, instead of pouring money down a rathole trying to "rehabilitate" hoodlums? Why not make it easier for ghetto youngsters to get jobs instead of easier for hustlers to get handouts?

It is slowly beginning to dawn on people that minimum wage laws price many youngsters out of a job—and lenient judges make crime a more attractive alternative. Add the irresponsible talk disdaining "menial" and "dead-end" jobs, and it is almost a miracle that there are still large numbers of minority youngsters out there playing it straight and making money the old-fashioned way.

Those hard-working youngsters are not headed for any dead-end. They are going to make it.

But our society may be headed for a dead-end in the long run if we don't start backing up the decent people, of all ages and races, instead of embracing the punks and bums who seem to fascinate deep thinkers in the media and academia.

—May 20, 1985

II

FOREIGN POLICY

Third World-ism

The image of the Third World in the West is one of pervasive poverty and ignorance. According to this stereotype, what is needed is more money from the West, and Western experts and planners to supply know-how and direction.

Few people notice that those who say this are often themselves Western "experts" and planners, and that they will be well paid out of the money they urge us to give.

Loose expressions like "the Third World" conceal more than they reveal. Countries lumped together under this label differ enormously. Even within a given country, there are often very prosperous areas and classes, along with destitution elsewhere.

The streets of New Delhi are far better paved than the streets of New York. So are the streets of Kuala Lumpur, in Malaysia. Many Third World governments own their own national airlines, whether they can afford them or not. Many projects, from steel mills to subways, are built for prestige rather than productivity.

The affluent classes in Third World countries often live with a magnificence that the average American can never hope to achieve. These are precisely the classes most likely to get their hands on American tax dollars sent overseas.

Some Third World governments simply buy what they want and beg for what they need. The government of India has built an air-conditioned sports stadium, seating 75,000 fans. Other Third World governments have built spectacular government buildings, or even whole new capital cities, while being subsidized by foreign aid.

Their hungry children can always be fed by contributions from America, or by international agencies.

The waste of material resources is only part of the story.

The waste of human resources is even more tragic. Many Third World nations contain very enterprising and productive individuals, classes, or racial and ethnic groups, perfectly capable of advancing the country to higher economic levels. An incredible amount of government effort goes into suppressing such people.

Politically unpopular minorities in many countries have been forbidden to engage in various economic activities, because their efficiency makes it difficult for others to compete with them. This has happened to the Chinese minority in the Philippines, Malaysia, and Indonesia, to the Lebanese in parts of Africa, and to others elsewhere.

Even in a country like India, where hunger and starvation have scarred their history, groups that produce far more food per acre than others are seen politically as competitive threats, rather than as boons to the nation. The Andras in the south of India and the Sikhs in the north are both resented because of their prowess as farmers and their economic success in general.

Much of the money already sent to the Third World has served to insulate politicians from the consequences of their own disastrous policies. Worse, it rewards doing things that don't work. Third World governments that have spent lavishly with borrowed money will be bailed out, while equally poor countries that lived within their means and followed more cautious policies lose out on this largesse.

Humanitarian aid, such as is now desperately needed to save the starving people of Ethiopia, is one thing. But that is not what most foreign aid is all about.

Foreign aid is the instrument by which the self-anointed, who want to plan and direct other people's lives at home, can do the same thing on a world scale. Sweeping social experiments have been supported by foreign aid, from Tanzania to Sri Lanka.

Too often these grand schemes have had the same counterproductive effects abroad that they have at home. African nations that have fed themselves for centuries, and sometimes exported food, now find themselves hungry after agricultural planning schemes have backfired again and again. Precisely after increased foreign aid was poured into Africa, its food production declined.

Many of the problems of the poorer nations, which foreign aid has helped aggravate, are now used as an excuse for a new massive crusade—against "overpopulation." The cold fact is that thinly populated nations are starving just as much as heavily populated nations. But any attempts to talk sense or facts about population are drowned out amid cries of outrage and impatience to "solve" the population "problem." A few more billion of our tax dollars, and the "experts" will be off and running again.

The whole vision of the world expressed in Third World-ism has become a crusade—which means that facts don't matter and moral posturing is where it's at.

—November 20, 1984

The World War II Anniversary

The fortieth anniversary of the end of World War II will bring many reminders of how it ended. We also need to remember how it started—especially if we don't ever want to see another world war.

The grand illusion of the 1930s was that wars grew out of misunderstandings, rather than calculated aggression. The "fears and suspicions" of "both sides" had to be put to rest by "personal contact" between their leaders, according to British Prime Minister Neville Chamberlain—the leading figure in the foreign policy of democratic nations at that time.

Chamberlain practically invented the notion of repeated summit conferences as the road to peace. Heads of state had met before, on ceremonial occasions, or in extraordinary negotiations at Versailles in 1918 or Vienna in 1812. But these were one-shot meetings. Chamberlain surprised and even shocked his contemporaries by repeatedly flying to continental Europe to confer with Hitler, Mussolini, and others.

Chamberlain's theory was that the "causes" of war had to be removed. That meant making concessions, signing agreements, and avoiding public criticisms that could be considered "inflammatory" by an adversary. He spoke in neutral terms about the German and Italian military intervention in the Spanish civil war, about Germany's brutal takeover of Austria, and about Italy's savage subjugation of Ethiopia. All were accepted as "facts of life," to which Britain had to adjust. Each crisis was viewed in isolation, with little or no thought as to what it revealed about the designs of the Nazi and fascist dictators.

Chamberlain called no one an "evil empire." On the contrary, he declared in 1937 that "there is not a country or a government that wants a European war." A year later—and just one year before war began—he still spoke of "the desire of the German people for peace." No doubt the German people did want peace, as the Soviet people want peace today. What Chamberlain failed to see was that this was totally irrelevant to the calculations of dictators.

In a world still haunted by the carnage of World War I, much as we are haunted by Vietnam today, Chamberlain's approach was the popular one. Few other British politicians seriously challenged him. One who did was Winston Churchill.

As early as 1932, Churchill warned of the "inexhaustible gullibility" of Western pacifists. Far from believing that the "causes" of war could be removed by concessions, he pointed out that "every concession that has been made" was only "followed immediately by fresh demands." He recognized the political pressures within Britain for disarmament but saw that as the road to war. "Britain's hour of weakness is Europe's hour of danger," he warned.

To those who proclaimed the horrors of modern warfare, Churchill replied that a country "cannot avoid war by dilating upon its horrors," but only by "deterrents against the aggressor." Churchill's warnings were ignored for seven long years. He was ridiculed and denounced in the press. A committee of his constituents barely missed voting censure of him in 1938.

Only after Nazi bombs were falling on Britain did they turn to Churchill to lead the country through the grim and desperate years ahead. No one expected Britain to survive—and it had a narrow escape. So did the Western world.

The great majestic words of Winston Churchill in those tragic times have been preserved in many places. We also need to look back at the words of Neville Chamberlain, for they reveal the kind of thinking that led to catastrophe. Chamberlain's book, *In Search of Peace*, should be required reading. It has all the clichés of today's so-called "peace" movement—and it turned out to be a road map to war.

—August 5, 1985

Wars of National Liberation

W ords too often mean the exact opposite of what they say. When bands of murderers shoot their way to political power and subjugate the people under a new tyranny, such actions are often called "wars of national liberation."

When the murderers need help to keep their own people subjugated, they may call on the Soviets for equipment and "advisors." With these Soviet advisors often come soldiers from Cuba, a member of the "non-aligned" nations.

If the people try to get rid of the regime imposed on them and Americans give them any money or equipment, that is called "imperialism." It is sure to provoke signs saying, "U.S. out of ——" wherever.

This farce reached its peak a couple of years ago, when the United States was denounced around the world for sending troops into Grenada—troops that were being cheered in the streets by the Grenadians. Numerous petty tyrants in the Third World had their representatives at the United Nations condemn the U.S. What these various little tyrants say is known as "world opinion," and Western democracies bend over backward to placate it.

Many of our European "allies" fell in line with "world opinion." American U.N. Ambassador Jeane Kirkpatrick reported that some of her U.N. colleagues congratulated her privately on what the U.S. had done in Grenada—just before voting publicly to condemn us.

Deep thinkers in the media and academia like to say that the "wars of national liberation" are "indigenous," that they cannot be treated as mere Communist expansionism. Like so much that is said by deep thinkers, it sounds terribly sophisticated the first time you hear it. It is only when you stop and think about it that its phoniness becomes apparent.

At this very moment, there are "indigenous" American revolutionists of the far left, the far right, and just plain crazies. If any one of these groups were to shoot their way to power in Washington, they could make exactly the same claim as those who conduct so-called "wars of national liberation" elsewhere. So what if we were "liberated" by people with foreign backing or a little help from foreign advisors? Deep thinkers would say the magic word, "indigenous," and everything would be all right.

There are disaffected elements and power-seekers in countries around the world. Unless human nature changes drastically from what it has been for the past few thousand years, there probably always will be.

Genuine local issues will of course be used by those seeking power. Many intergroup tensions and hostilities in various countries go back before there was a Soviet Union, or before Karl Marx was born. But the availability of massive Soviet aid and Cuban troops can be the difference between muttering in the coffee houses and murdering in the streets.

Deep thinkers are quick to point to abuses and injustices in various societies attacked by Soviet-backed "liberators." Abuses and injustices go back at least as far as recorded human history. If the only societies that can morally defend themselves are those with no abuses or injustices, then we may as well throw in the towel and tell the Soviets to take it all.

The degree of freedom, prosperity, and opportunity achieved in the United States and a handful of other nations is a rare and recent phenomenon in the history of this planet. Why it happened in these few places is by no means crystal clear. What is clear is that these free nations are the exceptions rather than the rule. Must all other nations be thrown to the wolves because they are not in our image?

In the brutal struggles of a civil war, you may rest assured that both sides will do things that turn the stomachs of decent people. Deep thinkers are preoccupied with seeing that the side we support plays by the Marquis of Queensberry rules, while the other side is kicking them in the groin.

Apparently it matters not whether you win or lose but how you play the game. That's not what Vince Lombardi said, and it's not what anyone will say when fighting for his life. But it's what you can say from the distant safety of an editorial office, or an academic campus, or a trendy pulpit.

"What is the difference between a Communist tyranny and any other kind of tyranny?" the moralizers ask. For one thing, Communist nations become military bases for further expansion. It is the difference between an infectious and a non-infectious disease. That's a big difference to people who value their health.

Another difference is that Communist tyranny is permanent, Grenada being the lone exception. Military juntas come and go in Latin America. Even fascism gave way to democracy in Spain, after the death of Franco. But Communism is a system that continues its grip, as its leaders come and go.

The biggest moral difference between Communism and other undemocratic systems is that no other systems cause so many millions of people to take desperate gambles with their lives to escape. That says it all.

—June 10, 1985

Reagan, Germans, and Jews

The furor over President Reagan's visit to Bitburg reflected very little credit on any of those involved—the president and his staff, his political enemies, the media, or the German government. In the process, some legitimate and important concerns were obscured and even set back.

The purpose of the trip was to symbolize and cement the solidarity of the Western democracies in general and especially of the new democratic and prosperous West Germany. For bitter enemies in two world wars to reconcile is a cause for rejoicing, not only by those nations, but by all who value peace in the world.

For a country without a strong democratic tradition to repudiate Nazism and emerge as one of the leading democratic nations in the world is also a cause for rejoicing. And for a nation to rise from the ashes and rubble of World War II to become a prosperous and a free people is a heartwarming story in a world too often darkened by tragedy.

The fortieth anniversary of the end of World War II was a fitting time to celebrate these historic achievements and to solidify the alliance of Western democratic nations, on which the peace of the world depends. Instead, old wounds were opened in Germany and America, and new resentments and suspicions rekindled.

The initial decision to by-pass the Nazi death camps was one of those incredible and outrageous things that can happen in Washington when political advisors get too clever for their own good. For this was also the fortieth anniversary of the liberation of skeleton-like survivors of one of the most monstrous events in human history—the Holocaust.

The victims were Jews but it was a crime against humanity. The tortures and soul-searing humiliations inflicted on millions of defenseless men, women, and children before they were murdered in cold blood was an obscene mockery of everything that civilization is supposed to stand for. Thousands of years of efforts to raise man above the animals were repudiated by the Nazis, whose savagery and sadism put them below the animals.

To the credit of today's German government, they included a visit to a concentration camp in the itinerary they suggested to the president. The clever people in Washington vetoed it. It wasn't upbeat. This was the kind of short-sighted narrowness that passes for "realism" in politics.

Add to this the casual inclusion of a Nazi military cemetery in the itinerary by presidential aides, preoccupied with buying themselves German cars at cut rates, and you have all the ingredients of a political disaster—not just for the president but for the Western alliance.

But ingredients do not mix themselves. Media hype, political sniping, presidential words in bad taste, and the German government's stubborn insistence on the Bitburg visit, all stirred the witches' brew.

One of the few people to bring credit on himself in all of this was Elie Wiesel, historian of the Holocaust. While making his impassioned plea for the president not to honor the site where Nazi SS men were buried, his were the thoughtful and dignified words of sorrow, tempered by an understanding of today's political imperatives for Western world unity. Wiesel rejected any suggestion of collective guilt on today's German generation for the sins of the past. He took none of the cheap shots of the media.

It would have been an honorable performance for anyone. It was majestic for someone who had himself been an inmate of a Nazi concentration camp.

Most of the Germans alive today were not even born at the time of Hitler and the Holocaust. The burden of historic tragedies beyond their control must at some point be lifted from the shoulders of this generation of human beings. President Reagan tried to say this, but his words came dangerously close to exonerating the Germany of the past instead of the present. His references to "one man" behind the evils of Nazi Germany and his equating of drafted German soldiers with Holocaust victims were reckless rhetoric in an already bad situation.

Today's Germans justly resent being thought of as Nazis. Part of the media flak aimed at Reagan has hit them. For too long it has been suggested that Nazi genocide reflected something basic in the German character. For forty years many who thought this way have been looking for a resurgence of Nazism that has not come. An ideology that left Germans starving amid the ruins and Germany torn in half is unlikely to have mass appeal.

The historic irony is that Germany was, for generations before Hitler, less anti-Semitic than much of the rest of Europe. It was a country to which persecuted Jews fled for refuge. Before the Nazis came to power, 20 percent of all the Jews in Germany were refugees from Eastern Europe. Jewish immigrants in other countries took part in the cultural life of German immigrants in those countries.

This added a special tragedy for Jews around the world when the hypnotic idiocy of Nazism swept over Germans. While Hitler never had a majority in a free election in Germany, he nevertheless had enormous support, both at home and abroad. There were flourishing Nazi movements among Germans as far away as Australia and Brazil. It was not just "one man" and his evil, as Reagan's rhetoric suggested.

That this could happen to a people less racist than many others has frightening implications. If it was a special problem of German character, the rest of us might relax. But the story of the Holocaust was not just a story about Germans and Jews. It is an ever-relevant story of deep and tragic flaws in man. It is for all of us to say: "Never again."

—May 7, 1985

The U.N. Promotes War—Not Peace

A remarkable shock greeted the suggestion that the United Nations could move elsewhere if its members did not like the United States as a host country. The American delegate, Charles M. Lichenstein, made the suggestion in response to testy remarks by the Soviet delegation. Like any straightforward statement in international affairs, it was later "clarified" by higher officials, so that it is now anybody's guess what American policy is.

The shock and the "clarification" both show that the United Nations is still a sacred cow in many places. Yet it would be hard to point to any concrete achievements of the United Nations that would justify such horror at the mere thought that it might relocate.

Even if the United Nations went out of existence, most of its non-political, humanitarian activities could be carried on by other international philanthropic organizations, or by the existing U.N. agencies operating independently. What does the United Nations do in its central, political forum that adds to the well-being of the world?

There is some vague notion abroad that the United Nations is a force for peace. If you judge by rhetoric, that may sound plausible. But if you judge by realities, the United Nations is more of a force for war. While there is much talk about the danger that war may occur inadvertently, most wars are deliberate, calculated risks. How does the United Nations affect such calculations? It reduces the risk to an aggressor.

Among the factors that an aggressor must take into account are the possibilities of his victim's resistance and retaliation. These may include not only repelling his attacks, but also responding with attacks on his territory, invasion of his country and the conquest and destruction of his government and perhaps himself. Before launching an attack, the aggressor must weigh the chances of these possibilities, which include his ending up dangling from a gallows, like the Nazis at Nuremberg.

The United Nations reduces the chances of all these possibilities, thereby making aggression a safer risk—especially when the victim is a democratic nation.

Nothing is more predictable in any war today than a U.N. call for a "cease-fire" and "negotiations." Non-democratic aggressors, like the Soviets in Afghanistan or the Syrians in Lebanon, ignore such calls with impunity. But in democratic nations, the political weight of this call from "world opinion" cannot always be brushed aside.

This has made aggression a game of heads-I-win and tails-we-tie. When the aggression succeeds, the aggressor carries it as far as he wants to. But when he encounters more resistance than he bargained for, the United Nations cuts his losses for him. A defending democratic nation cannot carry the war back to him and destroy his regime— much less hang him as he deserves. Long before that point, repeated U.N. calls for "peace," "compromise" and "humanity" will save his neck and leave him free to try again later.

At one time, an Argentine attack on the Falkland islands would have run the risk of British forces bombing and shelling Buenos Aires, if not invading and conquering Argentina. The Argentines knew that no such suicidal risk is involved these days. In fact, according to well-placed sources, the government even expected international political pressures to prevent Britain from retaking the islands. This was a miscalculation, but a small one, and the military government in Argentina is still in control of a physically unscathed nation. Stories are already appearing that they are developing a nuclear weapon for their next try.

In the Middle East, the Palestine Liberation Organization may declare all-out war on Israel, but Israel cannot conduct all-out war on the PLO. The voices of "peace" prevent it. Even if Israel is prepared to ignore the United Nations, it cannot completely ignore the United States, which has many ways to save the hide of aggressors in response to "world opinion." Even when the victims are American Marines in Lebanon, aggression has become a much safer occupation.

Part of this is due to the United Nations. Part of it is also due to our taking the United Nations far too seriously.

—September 29, 1983

South Africa

The bloody violence unleashed by African mobs against the Indians in South Africa should cause some second thoughts about the neat little morality play we have been hearing for so long about the tragic situation in that country.

Apartheid is so clearly the most hateful racism in the world since the Nazis that it was tailor-made to attract deep thinkers who see everything in terms of lining up on the side of the angels and imposing "solutions." But reality simply does not fit that pretty picture.

Neither the blacks nor the whites in South Africa are one people. In addition, there are Asians (mostly of Indian origin) and a mixed "colored" population that combines all three other racial groups. Tribal differences divide the black majority, and the whites are both ethnically and politically divided. As the wanton violence against the Indians shows, race hatred is by no means confined to whites.

The cast of characters in this tangled story also includes "world opinion"—meaning essentially foreign intellectuals, far removed from the scene and even farther removed from responsibility for the consequences of the policies they advocate. The painful complexities of trying to make a viable nation out of such disparate peoples, living in different centuries as well as in different racial and cultural worlds, are readily resolved by intellectuals with four magic words: "One man, one vote."

The failure of this formula all over Africa leaves deep thinkers unfazed. So many initially democratic African nations have so quickly become bloody despotisms that a cynical phrase has developed: "One man, one vote—one time."

But what actually happens to flesh-and-blood Africans (including 300,000 slaughtered by Idi Amin's regime alone) means much less to foreign intellectuals than being in favor of fashionable shibboleths. Nothing so epitomizes the tragedy of Africa as the fact that vast numbers of blacks continue to migrate into South Africa, because things are even worse in so many other African countries.

This migration of blacks into South Africa goes back well before the famines that have struck various parts of the continent in recent years. Moreover, these famines are by no means all due to droughts or other natural conditions. Food production has gone down even in some parts of Africa where the rainfall has been normal.

Disastrous economic experiments, based on the ideas of Western intellectuals, have added greatly to Africa's food shortages—even in countries that used to feed themselves and export the surplus. Attempts to impose political institutions peculiar to Western Europeans have likewise collapsed into anarchy, bloodshed, and tyranny in Africa. Undaunted, many deep thinkers are now convinced that Americans can impose some solution in South Africa from 10,000 miles away, even though we cannot solve our own budget deficit.

For too long, Africans have been used as guinea pigs for ideas that sounded good in Europe or America. The current fashion of "divestiture" is only the latest in a long series. If divestiture became effective, it would mean that many thousands of blacks in South Africa would lose their jobs, so that middle-class whites in America could feel noble in their colleges and churches, and American politicians could get good publicity at no cost to themselves.

Foreign boycotts are notoriously ineffective for achieving their goals, however effective they may be for moral posturing. It would be far more impressive if the morally anointed would put their own bank accounts in escrow to take care of the survivors of any bloodbath, anarchy, and economic collapse that might occur in South Africa, if their bright ideas don't work out any better there than in some other parts of Africa.

The Reagan Administration's policy of "constructive engagement" in South Africa has been a big target of the deep thinkers. It so happens that a few small improvements have taken place in South Africa during the Reagan Administration, whether or not the administration's policy had anything to do with it. But critics would rather die than admit that possibility.

Apartheid began when Harry Truman was President of

the United States, and neither he nor Eisenhower, Kennedy, Johnson, Nixon, Ford, or Carter was able to change it. Yet deep thinkers act as if it is only sheer stubbornness on Reagan's part that prevents him from changing South Africa's policies.

To the morally anointed, "solutions" are out there waiting to be discovered, like eggs at an Easter egg hunt. South Africa is one of the least promising places for such optimism.

—August 12, 1985

A Dashing New Dictator

There is now a dashing new dictator in the Kremlin, and the press is all aflutter.

Personally, I am sorry that Andrei Gromyko was not named head of the Soviet government. We have been seeing his sour face for about 40 years now, so it would be much harder to kid ourselves into believing that he is some nice fellow who is going to make everything all right.

Wishful thinking has been the curse of the Western democracies for most of this century. We got into World War II because we hoped for the best instead of maintaining a military deterrent.

But we learned nothing from that experience.

Since World War II, we have looked hopefully at each new Soviet dictator, as representing a turning point for peace and goodwill. This even included Andropov, who headed the KGB, where terror and torture are all in a day's work.

We thought Khrushchev had a certain rough charm. He sneaked nuclear missiles into Cuba and built the Berlin wall, in violation of both international agreements and common decency.

Some even called Josef Stalin "Uncle Joe." The people he killed ran into the millions.

Now the same thing is starting with Mikhail Gorbachev. People are already oooh-ing and aah-ing over his classy appearance and likening his wife to Jackie Kennedy. His smoothness has impressed the media.

Whether the prisoners in the Gulag are equally impressed is another question. The people being slaughtered in Afghanistan may well miss the deep significance of Gorbachev's tailoring or his wife's chic.

But the media will play it for all it is worth. They are great at dramatizing the little picture.

The big picture is that we are engaged in a long and deadly game of chess with the Soviet Union—and impatient chess players seldom survive. The nuclear submarines of both superpowers prowl every sea and hide under polar ice caps with their missiles aimed at each other's cities. We watch each other like hawks from our satellites, every hour of the day and night.

Gushing over Gorbachev seems a little out of place against this grim background.

The stakes the Soviets are playing for are the stakes they have always played for—an expanding empire. The stakes we are playing for are our own survival and the survival of freedom. The Soviets don't have a damn thing we want or need.

The Soviets are not reckless enough to try to win this international chess game by gambling on one big move. But if they can pick up small advantages here and there over the years, they may eventually be able to force us into a position that is indefensible.

If they ever maneuver into position to cut off Middle East oil, Europe is as good as theirs. If they can fill Latin America with new Cubas, or gain control of the strategic minerals of South Africa, we are in big trouble. If they can bankroll larger and larger amounts of terrorism around the world, the morale of the Western democracies may not be able to hold up in the long run.

With all our economic and scientific advantages over the Soviets, we have a weakness for short-run thinking. Congress doesn't want to spend money on long-range defense when that same money could be used to buy votes in the farm states today, or to keep campaign contributions coming in from the National Education Association.

In a world where democracy is a rare and recent achievement, it is easy to discredit American allies who haven't gotten there yet. This is a favorite political ploy of those who want to use defense money for vote buying instead.

They also talk about being "fair" when we cut back giveaway programs, by also cutting back the defense budget. How can you be "fair" to your own survival?

Gorbachev is tailor-made for these people, and vice versa. All he has to do is smile and sign pieces of paper, so Congress can cut back on defense and hand out more subsidies to special interests.

It won't even be disastrous immediately. But Gorbachev can take another of our pieces off the chess board and continue the game. A totalitarian regime can take the long view.

It may not be us, but our children, who will be forced to decide whether it is better to be red than dead.

—March 15, 1985

Buthelezi in South Africa

The jerry-built shanties which have been springing up on American college campuses to urge disinvestment in South Africa are a perfect symbol of the students' hastily thrown-together thinking about the complex, tragic and potentially catastrophic situation in that country. Students and the media alike seem to want to reduce it all to a simple morality play, and to be on the side of "the good guys" against "the bad guys."

That's fine if your own moral posturing is paramount, with the fate of 24 million human beings in South Africa being secondary. But recent outbreaks of violence of blacks against blacks and whites against whites in South Africa give a glimpse of underlying cross-currents which make a mockery of attempts to see that country's troubles in simple terms. Both blacks and whites are severely divided internally, and there is also an important Indian community and a Colored community, each with its own distinct interests and strong feelings.

The two main white groups—the Afrikaners and the British—fought two very ugly and agonizing civil wars against each other. Anyone aware of how many generations of smoldering resentments followed the American Civil War cannot under-estimate what that means—especially since the civil wars in South Africa were more recent. Now the Afrikaners, long the strongest supporters of apartheid, have begun to split among themselves over the economic costs and political dangers created by this system of racial oppression, which has provoked such hatred and resistance from blacks.

But blacks in South Africa are also far from united.

66

Tribal enmities go back in history to the subjugation of some tribes by others, before the whites arrived to subjugate them all. Recent militant campaigns against the South African government have created murderous rivalries among blacks with different agendas and different turf. One of the many bitter consequences of oppression is to legitimize anarchy among the oppressed. Mutual slaughters and atrocities among blacks have taken far more lives than those lost in black-white confrontations.

In short, South Africa's deep divisions within and between groups provide all the ingredients of a "war of each against all," if the present regime is toppled before there is a viable alternative with enough support to govern. One man who is keenly aware of this possibility is Zulu Chief Gatsha Buthelezi. "Bloody revolutions fought against terrible oppression do not automatically bring about great improvements," Buthelezi has said. This has certainly been the history of the French Revolution, the Bolshevik Revolution, and such African revolutions as those which brought to power Idi Amin in Uganda and the current Communist government of Ethiopia.

Although Buthelezi is the leader of the largest single group in South Africa—more than 5 million Zulus—he has been largely ignored by the American media. They prefer to feature Bishop Desmond Tutu, whose emotional and symbolic approach is far more suited to television— and to morality plays—than is the skeptical and low-key analysis of Buthelezi.

While Tutu urges disinvestment as the answer to apartheid, Buthelezi wants more foreign investment as a source not only of jobs and skills for blacks, but also as a force eroding apartheid in American-owned and European-owned firms.

Chief Buthelezi's attempt to walk a political tightrope— opposing apartheid but also opposing violence and disinvestment—makes him an easy target for the cheap shot that he has sold out to the white South African government. CBS newsman Ed Bradley went for this cheap shot on a recent "60 Minutes" program. In an interview ostensibly for the purpose of getting Buthelezi's views on South Africa, Bradley's whole tone was accusatory from the outset, and it quickly became clear that the real issue was Buthelezi and whether he was for real.

As the program was aired, Buthelezi's replies were spliced together with sneering rejoinders from his political enemies. The viewer was not told that one of these enemies who repeatedly spoke of Buthelezi with such moral disdain, Reverend Allan Boesak, had himself barely managed to retain his ministry after his own scandals came to light.

Chief Buthelezi has been considered by some to be one of the wisest men in South Africa, and one of the few individuals with enough support among both blacks and whites to hold out some hope of a transition to a better society rather than a bloodbath. But he was clearly unfamiliar with the strange tribal customs of American television.

Apparently beginning the "60 Minutes" interview with the idea that the subject was South Africa, Buthelezi seemed momentarily baffled by the strange turn of Bradley's questioning. It was a classic case of bait-and-switch journalism—a "gotcha."

Cute journalistic tricks don't seem quite as cute against the tragic background of South Africa. No one knows at this juncture whether the strategy of Buthelezi, of the Mandelas, or of Bishop Tutu will work—or if anything will work in South Africa. We need to hear a variety of views and strategies—not have CBS and "60 Minutes" decide for us who is to be the "real" voice of blacks and who is to be smeared rather than heard.

—June 9, 1986

Denying Aid to the Contras

Congress has once more disgraced itself. The House of Representatives' vote to turn down military aid to the Contra forces opposing the Sandinistas in Nicaragua is a cop-out heard round the world.

Vulnerable nations, political movements, and guerilla forces around the world have to decide how they are going to align themselves internationally in order to survive in a world where two rival nations have overwhelming power. The House of Representatives has sent them the message that the United States is an unreliable support in a time of crisis. They already know that the Soviets are a very reliable support for countries and movements that line up with them. The Soviets will not only pour in military supplies but will also fight to the last Cuban.

Nothing is more pathetic, more fatuous, or more dishonest than the claim that we should rely on "negotiation" rather than force to resolve the conflict in Nicaragua, and the threat Nicaragua poses to its neighbors. Nobody negotiates for the sheer pleasure of negotiation. In international power politics, trying to negotiate without force is like trying to buy without money or eat without food. A gunman does not negotiate with an unarmed victim, though he may negotiate when the police surround his hideout.

Force is the reason for negotiations. This is one of the brutal realities of international power politics, from which too many Americans try to escape into a dream world.

We live in an international jungle, where beasts of prey eat the weak, and where only the strong or the wary survive. Angola is ruled by a Marxist regime today, not because Angolans wanted it, but because the Soviets sent in 20,000 Cuban troops to support the Marxist minority, while the United States played Hamlet over whether to support the anti-Communist forces, even with financial aid.

If we keep repeating this scenario over the years, it is only a matter of time before Soviet satellite nations cover the globe. Historians of a thousand years from now may be baffled as to how this could have happened, with the Soviet Union so far behind the United States economically, in science and technology, and with a miserable Communist society from which people seek to escape even at the risk of their lives.

The kind of thinking—or wishing—behind the House vote to deny financial aid to anti-Communist guerillas in Nicaragua may provide a clue to Soviet penetration into Africa, the Caribbean, the Middle East—and now the mainland of Central America. All around the world, the Soviets are positioning themselves, on land and at sea, across the vital supply lines of oil and other materials on which the survival of Western civilization depends.

Meanwhile, we are talking pretty talk and copping out. International organizations devoted to empty rhetoric help us maintain our illusions. The United Nations is the foremost of the organizations playing this farcical but ultimately tragic role. However, ineffective regional groupings of countries, such as the Latin "contadora" nations, also serve the same function of making vacillation sound noble. Those who voted against supporting the Contras often referred loftily to letting "the contadora peace process" work. Sure, Mac.

There is a lot of talk about the "lessons of Vietnam." Many of those who talk this way were the very people who made it impossible for the United States to bring that war to an end sooner, and victoriously. They insisted that we not bomb here, or mine there, or invade enemy territory, and—above all—that we "negotiate." American lives must never be put on the line again under these political conditions. The real lesson of Vietnam is that weaker forces with determination win over stronger forces that vacillate. Yet Vietnam is now used as a reason to vacillate again in Central America.

No one wants American troops to be sent to fight other people's battles for them. But the brutal oppressions of Communism have caused many peoples, in many parts of the world, to put their own lives on the line against it, even while Marxist rhetoric continues to fascinate Western intellectuals.

What those people need from us are not our young men but military supplies costing much less than even small and wasteful social programs. All of the noise about military aid to the Contras concerned a sum of money less than one-fifth of what the same Congress proposes to spend subsidizing one variety of tobacco.

The real objection to any military spending—at home or abroad—is that it reduces the amount of money available to give away buying votes. The big spenders on social programs are always opposed to military spending. They are the first to criticize our allies for not being noble enough to deserve our support. It is a very effective political strategy for the short run—and the next election is what political strategy is all about.

In the longer run, this political cleverness can mean that we leave posterity not only with a huge national debt and uncovered liabilities for Social Security, but also surrounded by Communist nations.

—March 24, 1986

The Lessons of Pearl Harbor

Why do we keep remembering Pearl Harbor, after all these years?

To anyone old enough to recall December 7, 1941, the very question may seem odd. The Japanese attack on Pearl Harbor was a shattering event in everyone's life, and it changed this nation overnight. Indeed, the whole world would never be the same again.

But for most of the people in the world today, Pearl Harbor is just a name in the history books. Considering how so much history is taught—with America and the West assumed to be wrong from the outset—it is especially important that the current generation understand the lesson of Pearl Harbor.

All the things that are being advocated by the "peace movement" today were tried in the 1920s and 1930s. That is what led to war.

We came dangerously close to losing that war—and with it losing everything decent in Western civilization. The sickening barbarism of Hitler and the Nazis we know all too well. The Japan of that era was more of the same, and very different from the peaceful, democratic Japan of today.

Hiroshima and Nagasaki had a lot to do with that change.

The long road to Pearl Harbor began back in the 1920s. Peace and disarmament were the prime concerns of the world, after the horrors of World War I. The United States and Britain began sinking their own warships as their contribution toward world peace.

That made the growing Japanese navy even more powerful. The weakness of Western forces, and the weakness of attitude that caused it, provided Japan with the fatal temptation to strike.

The Japanese were not reckless. They tested their growing strength with invasions of Manchuria and China. And they watched how the West responded.

The West did nothing. It did not even rearm.

It was the same story in Europe. As Hitler began assembling a massive war machine in the 1930s, the Western democracies made little effort to defend themselves. Militant "peace" movements throughout the democratic world made it politically impossible to rearm on a scale that would deter aggression.

Anyone who supported beefed-up defenses was denounced as a war monger, a promoter of an "arms race" or of the munitions industry. An effort was even made to get Winston Churchill recalled from Parliament for advocating more military defense.

In the Pacific the sleek, new Japanese navy was a growing contrast to the aging ships of the U.S. Navy. The U.S. Army had few troops, pathetically ill-equipped.

The treacherous and devastating attack on Pearl Harbor—right in the middle of negotiations—was the payoff to two decades of illusions. The war already under way in Europe was now truly a Second World War.

All over the world, young men paid with their lives for the moral posturing of clergymen and editorial writers who had long advocated peace through disarmament. The "peace" movement never understood that the only one you can disarm is yourself.

Pearl Harbor had another tragic lesson, of lasting importance.

The Japanese had no illusions that they could match the industrial and military power of the United States when they bombed Pearl Harbor. But they didn't think we had the guts for a long war. Everything we had done up to that point made this look like a good gamble.

Maybe the Japanese would be right today. With television bringing the gore of war into every home, and mournful pundits undermining morale, maybe we wouldn't be able to go on.

But in 1941, the attack on Pearl Harbor provoked an instant realization of what fools we had been. "Remember Pearl Harbor!" became a rallying cry that kept us going as our young men bled and died all across the Pacific.

A young naval officer named John F. Kennedy nearly lost his life in that war. He never forgot its lesson. As president, he said: "We dare not tempt them with weakness."

Ronald Reagan may be the last American president who can personally remember Pearl Harbor. But if the nation ever forgets its lesson, we may not be able to remember the next Pearl Harbor.

—November 28, 1984

Disinvestment in South Africa

Divestment in South Africa has become a political crusade—which is to say, there is no point trying to talk sense to those who believe in it. Policies are judged by their consequences but crusades are judged by how good they make the crusaders feel.

The latest politician to cave in to the divestment crusaders is Governor George Deukmejian of California—who is running for re-election this year. After initially resisting pressures to divest, Deukmejian recently flip-flopped and threw his weight behind divestment of the vast holdings of the University of California in companies that do business in South Africa. The university stands to lose more than $100 million in brokerage fees alone.

How much will South Africa lose from all this? Not one dime. The fact that stock certificates once held by one set of Americans will now be held by a different set of Americans is no skin off their nose.

Moves are already afoot to divest from state employees' pension funds as well. Vast financial losses can also be expected there, not only from brokerage fees but also from falling prices of the stocks as a huge supply of them is dumped on the market at one time. Part of the money put aside to support workers in their old age will be poured down the drain for political symbolism.

Not everybody is going to take this lying down. Unions representing the workers whose pension funds will be reduced are certain to file lawsuits. So can taxpayers. Trustees who betray their trust by doing things that they know will lose money from the funds entrusted to their care can be held legally responsible.

Those who are pushing divestment are now trying to get around this legal responsibility by introducing legislation to give trustees legal immunity. But whether the courts will let such legislation stand is a big question.

What is the point of having trustees if they can't be trusted with the money? Just as they are not allowed to dip into pension funds or university investments for their own financial gain, neither should they be allowed to spend that money to make themselves feel good or to gain political support at the next election.

If divestment were a policy rather than a crusade, it would be logical to ask who gains what and who loses what. Stock speculators who can buy the divested stock at reduced prices will make millions, if not billions. Taxpayers and pensioners will lose the same amounts—plus broker-age fees. The South African government loses nothing and South African blacks gain nothing. Politicians, college presidents, and assorted crusaders all gain image.

If you go beyond reshuffling of stock ownership to ac-tual removal of capital from South Africa, then there are real consequences—but not necessarily what you want. If an American corporation has built a factory in South Af-rica, and decides it is not worth the hassle and bad pub-licity to stay there, it can pull out—but it can't put the factory on a boat and bring it home. It has to sell the factory to someone.

Very few blacks in South Africa are in any position to buy a factory or any other American business there. Chances are it will be sold to South African whites or to the South African government—the very racist government that we claim to be trying to pressure. Whoever buys these disinvested properties will probably get them as bargains, because dumping a lot of investments at once will drive down the price. American and other foreign companies in South Africa have often provided blacks there with some of their best opportunities for skills, money, and better treatment. This is something well worth considering in any policy decision, though it is of course brushed aside by crusaders.

While divestment of existing stock certificates or disinvestment in existing capital equipment in South Af-rica imposes immediate losses only on those who do it, South Africa's loss of access to foreign sources of future investments and loans will undoubtedly have adverse ef-fects on that country's economy. What that means politi-cally is by no means clear.

South Africa's dwindling chances of a peaceful transi-tion to a better society depend upon some kind of mutual accomodation between those whites who are prepared to sacrifice apartheid and those blacks who want a better future for themselves and their children than they can get from a bloodbath or chaos.

It is hopelessly optimistic to expect the collapse of the Pretoria government, with or without disinvestment, and with or without more violence from the African National Congress or other revolutionary groups. The overwhelming military power of the white government, and its repeatedly demonstrated ruthlessness in using it, make the prospects of a black takeover by force nil, no matter how often it is predicted by wishful thinkers in the West.

The real choices in South Africa are mutual accommodation or a bloodbath and chaos. A siege mentality, heightened by economic isolation, is not a promising condition for moderate voices in both races to be heard or heeded. Only the Soviet Union or the Western media stand to gain from a bloodbath or chaos in South Africa.

The Soviets would gain because South Africa and the U.S.S.R. between them contain more than 90 percent of the world's supply of various strategic minerals, including uranium. It is no accident that terrorists in South Africa use Soviet weapons. That doesn't matter to the crusaders either.

—August 11, 1986

The Iceland Summit

Deep thinkers have been busy explaining the "failure" of the Iceland Summit. Liberals in the media and in politics have been especially disappointed, for they regard any agreement between the U.S. and the U.S.S.R. as a reason to cut the military budget and put that money into giveaway programs.

In reality, the Iceland summit may have been the most successful summit that the United States has ever had with the Soviet Union. Too often in the past, American leaders have signed one-sided deals with the Soviets, in order to come back with an agreement and call the meeting a "success." The euphoria surrounding these meetings has often lasted for months afterwards, under such labels as "the spirit of Geneva," "the spirit of Tashkent," "the spirit of Glassboro," or wherever else the meetings took place. In each case, it was only a matter of time before some new brutality by the Soviets brought us back to reality.

The fact that the "star wars" defense system prevented agreement in Iceland was very significant. The combination of large reductions in nuclear missiles and development of a system for shooting down the remaining missiles could have drastically reduced the possibility of a nuclear Pearl Harbor. But that would have meant drastically reducing the Soviets' ability to engage in nuclear blackmail against Western nations.

Those who sneer at "star wars" fail to understand its purpose. The purpose of a defense against nuclear missiles is not to win World War III, but to prevent World War III. Critics ask how we can be sure that any defense system will stop all the missiles headed our way after the Soviets push the nuclear button. The real question is how the Soviets can be sure enough of the outcome before they decide whether or not to push that button.

Wars can never be reduced to a certainty. Even a defense system that cannot stop all missiles may still leave the attacker wondering whether the ones that get through will hit New York, Chicago, and Los Angeles or the Rocky Mountains, the Southwest desert, and the Gulf of Mexico. And if they don't know whether our counter-attacking missiles that get through will land in the Siberian wastelands or in Leningrad and Moscow, then the whole gamble is too risky to launch an attack in the first place. The Soviets have never been reckless gamblers, much less suicidal.

"Star wars" does not have to achieve perfection to deter an attack. All it has to do is increase the uncertainty of the outcome to a point that makes a nuclear Pearl Harbor a bad gamble. This same uncertainty likewise protects the Soviets from any "first strike" attack from the United States.

If the Soviets' purpose was greater security for themselves, they would have taken President Reagan's offer and heaved a sigh of relief. But if their purpose is to use their huge nuclear arsenal for blackmailing other nations, "star wars" undermines their game plan.

The president's insistence on having both missile reductions and "star wars" was the logical position for a country that wants to prevent both nuclear war and nuclear blackmail. Merely reducing the number of missiles from a level that will kill everyone 10 times over to a level that will kill everyone 5 times over is not really accomplishing much. But, with a missile defense system, the crucial issue is reducing the number of missiles to a level too small to overwhelm the system's capacity.

The two things go together, and the president was right not to let the Soviets separate them. The Soviets now know that the President of the United States can say "no" to an agreement, even on the eve of elections—and that the American people back him up, as the polls demonstrate. Future presidents will also know that. They can refuse to be patsies just to get an agreement. That is why the Iceland summit can be historic as our first real success in the long series of meetings between Soviet and American leaders, going all the way back to Yalta.

—October 21, 1986

Two Tyrannies in South Africa

"**W**hat I have just said to you, I would not dare to say in my own country." A black South African spoke these words to me after explaining what life is like for him and others in one of the segregated townships of that nation.

He lives under two tyrannies, while the outside world thinks he lives under one. The oppression of the racist government of South Africa is well known. The ease with which they will uproot a whole community or fire into a crowd is a monument, not only to racism, but to the arrogance of power as well. What is not so well known is the reign of terror against blacks by other blacks, especially by the Soviet-backed African National Congress. More blacks are being killed by other blacks than by whites.

Hoodlums calling themselves "comrades" are the enforcers when a school boycott or rent strike is called for some political purpose. Those who dare to attend school or to pay their rent risk physical retaliation against themselves or their families. The black South African who spoke to me was well aware that such free discussion in his own township could bring a gasoline bomb to his home some night.

The "comrades" have developed an elaborate ritual for public executions. A tire, filled with gasoline, is placed around the victim's neck and set ablaze. It is called a "necklace." People like Winnie Mandela justify this as a punishment for "collaborators." But the history of terrorism suggests that anyone they want to do this to will simply be labelled a collaborator.

Bishop Desmond Tutu, after much hesitation, finally condemned "necklacing" recently. The "comrades" were furious.

Ironically, the white population of South Africa largely escapes the violence and terror of the urban guerilla movement, and lives a relatively normal and comfortable life. Apartheid is the symbolic target of the terrorists, but the flesh-and-blood targets are black people who do not do what they are told by their "liberators." The kind of dramatic showdown between the guerillas and the government that the American media seem to want in South Africa can mean simply changing the color of tyranny.

No doubt Winnie Mandela has good reason to be bitter against the South African government for its treatment of her and her imprisoned husband, Nelson Mandela. But it is all too easy to romanticize victims into heroes and liberators. Josef Stalin was imprisoned in Siberia by the czarist government. The Shah of Iran exiled the Ayatollah Khomeini. But when Stalin and Khomeini came to power, they were hardly liberators.

A black South African who is attempting to find another, more democratic path to ending apartheid is Chief M. G. Buthelezi. He was described to me years ago as the wisest man of any race in South Africa. My brief encounter with him during his recent visit to Stanford University reinforced that opinion.

Buthelezi's picture of South Africa confirmed what I had already been told by the black township resident and by others. Buthelezi has had to fight on two fronts—against "the repugnance of apartheid and its gross affront on Black human dignity" and against "the violent intimidation of Black people" by revolutionary terrorists. He has a penetrating mind and an inner toughness that shows through his low-key manner and quiet words. He will need all of that merely to survive in South Africa, much less to bring about a more democratic nation.

If he somehow manages to succeed, it will undoubtedly takes years, with irregular advances and setbacks, instead of the kind of dramatic confrontations dear to the heart of the media—and of demagogues. While Buthelezi leads the largest black political organization in South Africa, his influence is limited by the fact that his followers are disfranchised. His following among the more enlightened whites opens him to the charge of being a collaborator.

In addition to his domestic political enemies on the left and the right, Buthelezi faces foreign suspicion and hostility, especially since he has raised serious questions about the actual impact of Western divestment on black South Africans. During his visit to Stanford, a huge banner on campus called for an "uprising" to protest his presence.

For these affluent, over-privileged Stanford students to call for an "uprising," as if they were the downtrodden of Paris storming the Bastille, is a farce—but a tragic farce, in view of the desperate need for hearing as many views as possible on the explosive South African situation. Years from now, when today's campus demonstrator has become a middle-aged banker or advertising executive, with two Mercedes in his suburban driveway, he may look back with a chuckle on these demonstrations as one of the adventures of his youth. He may well have forgotten all about South Africa by then. And if some new tragedy there makes headlines, he may innocently wonder how it happened.

—December 8, 1986

The Iranian Arms Deal

No amount of public relations can camouflage the bitter fact that the United States paid ransom to Iran—again—to get hostages back. The zigzag channels through which this was done don't matter. What matters is that it was done—and that ransom guarantees that future hostages will be taken. This brutal reality has been evaded or ignored for seven long years, since the original Iranian hostage crisis under Jimmy Carter.

In each hostage situation, the prime focus of the media and the public has been on the fate of those individuals currently being held captive. These feelings do us credit as a people. There are countries where the slaughter of a thousand innocents is quietly accepted.

But feelings alone will not "solve" the "problem," as some like to phrase it. Ultimately there is no solution, but only a painful trade-off, between today's hostage and tomorrow's hostages, who will be seized if today's hostage is ransomed. Israeli hostages are seldom taken, for that is likely to bring retaliation instead of ransom. But an American government cannot follow such a policy as long as public opinion—and the media hype that feeds it—refuses to look beyond today's tragedy to tomorrow's tragedies, stretching on into the future.

President Carter set a pattern that is still being followed, when he made the fate of the original hostages his overriding priority. He built up the maximum political pressure on himself to get them back by publicly counting the days they were held and by other symbolic gestures. After painting himself into a corner, he had no choice but to ransom them, after his abortive rescue effort ended in a tragic fiasco.

None of this exonerates Ronald Reagan or his White House advisors. As a candidate for the presidency in 1980, Reagan criticized Carter's hostage policy and promised a different approach. He may well have meant it.

But the Washington atmosphere can have insidious effects on people's minds—especially by convincing them that clever is better. There is something about the underhanded use of power that makes it seem so shrewd, even when it is abysmally stupid.

This episode has cut the ground out from under the moral and political support needed for the painful, long-run task of fighting international terrorism. The very reason why a handful of third-rate powers and little bands of sadistic thugs can repeatedly win, against the much greater power of the Western world, is that the Western countries try to cop out with soft options, empty symbolism, and even with special undercover deals with terrorists.

It is hardly surprising for Greece to do this. What would you expect from a country headed by a former Berkeley professor? But for "hard-liner" Ronald Reagan to do it is something else. The old battle-cry "Let Reagan be Reagan," seems to have been superseded by more expediency-minded counsel in the White House.

Stupidity alone, however, cannot fully explain what has happened. There is only so much trouble that you are likely to get into through stupidity. Something that is simultaneously bungling, messy, disgraceful, and disastrous usually requires very clever people, working very hard at being clever.

Watergate was the classic example. People who know Richard Nixon have repeatedly marvelled at the man's brainpower. There have undoubtedly been less brainy presidents—who never brought any such unnecessary disaster down upon themselves.

Cleverness may be the occupational hazard of White House staffers, including the chief of staff, Donald Regan. Even as Secretary of the Treasury, Regan was master of that short-sighted cunning known in Washington as "practicality." In more than one area, the question has been raised whether the Ronald Reagan Administration has not become the Donald Regan Administration.

A much bigger question is whether the president has the stomach for a real house-cleaning in the White House staff, or whether he thinks that throwing a couple of lower-echelon staffers to the wolves will stop them from baying at his door.

—November 25, 1986

III

ECONOMICS

Bogeyman Economics

People may argue about Keynesian economics, monetarist economics, or supply-side economics. But the actual decisions made by politicians and judges are dominated by bogeyman economics.

It would be impossible to understand those travesties of logic known as anti-trust cases, without understanding the bogeymen hovering in the background of the judges' thinking. The hard evidence in many of these cases would not be enough to sustain a conviction for jay-walking. But a prosecutor who can weave together statistics and theories in such a way as to conjure up the specter of an outside chance of monopoly is well on his way to winning the case.

Courts have broken up mergers in which the two companies put together had less than 10 percent of the sales in the industry. One businessman convicted of an anti-trust violation had less than 20 employees and more than 70 competitors. When judges believe that such defendants can "substantially lessen competition," you are no longer talking about evidence and logic, but about paranoia and bogeymen.

One of the big alarums of recent years has been over "monopolization" of newspapers in many communities. In this era of nationally distributed newspapers like *USA Today,* the *New York Times,* and the *Wall Street Journal,* how anyone can monopolize the newspaper business in some local community is beyond me—but not beyond those who believe in bogeyman economics.

Currently, the Antitrust Division of the Justice Department is solemnly—or at least with a straight face—looking into a business deal among newspapers in Evansville, Indiana. The deal can go forward only after Justice Department approval, and they will approve only after they have satisfied themselves that the net result will not be a local newspaper monopoly. During a recent visit to Evansville, I found *USA Today* and the *Wall Street Journal* both available in the hotel lobby at 6 A.M.

In Palo Alto, California (population 50,000), you can get the *New York Times* and the *Wall Street Journal* delivered to your doorstep—or at least thrown in the general direction of the house. San Francisco and San Jose newspapers are also widely available in Palo Alto grocery stores, drugstores, and bookstores. Vending machines on the streets also sell these newspapers—plus Los Angeles and Sacramento papers and the *Christian Science Monitor*.

Statistically, however, Palo Alto is included among those blighted communities where one locally produced daily newspaper has a "monopoly." In reality, there has never been such a diversity of newspapers available all across the country—even in the boondocks—as during the present era of local newspaper "monopoly." Rapid transportation and electronic communication have vastly increased the area that can be served by a given newspaper, reducing the demand for locally produced papers. It is only when this simple economic fact is seen through a fog of bogeyman visions that political and legal hysteria is generated.

According to bogeyman economics, monopolies are a constant threat to jack up prices and "exploit" the consumer. The irony is that far more anti-trust cases have been prosecuted against companies for lowering prices than for raising prices. When a more efficient company cuts prices and its competitors lose business because they cannot afford to do the same, that is when they turn to the feds.

Some monopolies and cartels do in fact jack up prices beyond what they would be in a competitive market. But this is almost invariably with the help of government. Government-regulated and subsidized sectors—from agriculture to the maritime industry—charge prices far above what the market would tolerate, if politicians did not stifle competition.

One of the few genuine monopolies to arise independently of government was the Aluminum Company of America (Alcoa), which was the only producer of virgin ingot aluminum in the United States from the late nineteenth century until World War II. However, after half a century of Alcoa monopoly, the price of aluminum had fallen to less than one-tenth of what it was originally, and Alcoa's rate of profit was a modest 10 percent.

Why? Because many things that are made of aluminum could also be made of tin, steel, copper, wood, and many other materials. Potential substitutes reduce even a total monopoly's opportunity to act the way bogeyman economics expects. Competition does a much more effective job than government at protecting consumers.

—October 6, 1986

India and Hong Kong

What is smaller than Los Angeles and yet imports and exports more than India?

It is not a trick question. The answer is Hong Kong.

The population of India is well over a hundred times greater than the population of Hong Kong. India is a huge nation: From Bombay to Calcutta is farther than from London to Rome. Hong Kong is a few patches of land, centering around lovely Victoria Harbor, and adding up to barely 400 square miles.

How then does this little colony manage to send vast

quantities of its products around the world and prosper, while India remains a symbol of Third World poverty?

The cultures and histories of the two places are of course wholly different. But no one lives off history. They live off what they are currently doing. And what they are doing in India is very different from what they are doing in Hong Kong.

India is a land of pervasive government restrictions on economic activities. An Indian manufacturer cannot use more electricity to increase his output simply because he wants to and can pay for it. He must first become a supplicant to some bureaucrat, whose permission is needed, and who is in no hurry. The businessman's hiring policies or his general attitude may be assessed before the government condescends to let him use more electricity.

It is hardly surprising that corruption scandals abound under these conditions. Or that Indian products are so costly that they have trouble competing with foreign products, even within India, much less in the world market.

India is proud of producing its own automobiles, but the costs are so high that they dare not let foreign-made cars come in to compete. If you want a car in India, you must get on a waiting list—and not expect to drive it this year, or even next. There are many products that the government will not allow to be imported, because the Indian version is far more costly, or inferior in quality, or both.

Tourists coming into India are cross-examined as to whether they might be carrying a movie camera or even a pocket calculator. The Indian government is afraid that they might sell it—and there would be plenty of buyers.

Hong Kong is just the opposite. It is almost a textbook example of free enterprise. Practically anything can be imported. A Japanese firm even won the bidding to do some construction work for the Hong Kong government. If you want American film, a Swiss watch, or a Japanese stereo, just go into a store in Hong Kong and ask for it.

The price will probably be lower than it is where it is manufactured. Store signs that say "Duty Free" impress only the most naive tourist. All Hong Kong is duty free.

Tall new apartment buildings and business skyscrapers abound in Hong Kong. Government restrictions prevent that in Bombay or New Delhi, to protect the "quality of life." The net result in both Indian cities is a proliferation of shanty towns that stink to high heaven.

The tragic irony is that India produces many intelligent, talented, and enterprising people. Indians are very successful in other countries. Indians in Malaysia have long had higher incomes than the Malays. In some scientific fields in Malaysia, there are more Indians than Malays, even though Indians are only about 10 percent of the population. Indians also created much of the commercial and industrial life in a number of countries in east Africa, and at one time rupees were the common currency there. Indians earned several times the average income of Africans.

The success of Indians overseas has not been confined to Third World countries. The 1980 U.S. Census shows that the average person from India living in California earns more than the average white American living in California.

The talent is there. So are the Indian bureaucrats and politicians, to put obstacles in its path. Envy has become politically sanctified as "fairness" and "equality." In practice, that means keeping the productive from getting too far ahead of the unproductive. It also means holding India back.

—November 8, 1984

59 Percent Rhetoric

The classic rule of propaganda is that people will believe any lie, if it is repeated often enough, loud enough, and long enough. One of the major "facts" of our time has been created in just this way—the claim that a woman receives only 59 percent of what a man receives for doing the same work.

Reporters, interviewers, and talk show hosts (who mercilessly grill businessmen or politicians) roll over and play dead when this magic number is spoken. Guilt and denunciations of our evil society are the only acceptable responses to this vision of victimhood. Thinking is as out of place as mustard on a chocolate cake.

Like so many of the numbers that conjure up political visions, this 59 percent comes from adding apples and oranges. Women average far fewer hours of work per year than men, partly because women work part-time more so than men. Women also remain on a given job fewer years. This is especially true of married women, and particularly those with children.

None of this is hard to understand, given the competing demands on wives and mothers. What is hard to understand is why it is ignored by those who throw numbers around.

If you compare people who are comparable, an entirely different picture emerges. Among people who remain single, women earn 91 percent of the income of men. Nor can the other 9 percent automatically be called "discrimination." There are physically demanding and well-paid fields that women seldom enter—mining, lumberjacking and construction work, for example. There are other well-paying fields that require a mathematics background that most women do not have. These include not only engineering, chemistry and physics but also economics and other fields that are increasingly becoming mathematical.

Even with all of this, the difference in income between men and women is not very large, when comparing people who have never married. The big difference is between married women and everyone else.

Married women are far more likely to work part-time, to stop working altogether for various periods of time, or to take jobs whose hours and duties do not conflict with their responsibilities at home—even if these are not the highest paying jobs they could get.

It is not employer discrimination when those who work fewer hours are paid less. Or when those who are employed intermittently make less than those with years of continuous full-time experience.

Back in the early 1970s, a study showed that women in their thirties who had worked continuously since high school earned slightly *more* than men of the same description.

In the academic world, women who received their Ph.D.s in the 1930s—and never married—had become full professors in the 1950s to a slightly greater extent than men. This was before anyone had heard of "women's liberation."

Marriage has opposite effects on the incomes of men and women. While married women work less than single women, especially when there are children, married men work more than single men—also especially when there are children. There is nothing mysterious about this, for anyone who knows what it is to have more mouths to feed.

The net result is that there are huge differences between the incomes of married women and married men. Wives who are living with their husbands earn about one-fourth of the income of husbands who are living with their wives. Lump these wives together with the other women, and the husbands with other men, and you get the magic 59 percent.

Where the income differences are largest, there is the least likelihood that women live more poorly than men. When the husband is prosperous, the wife is not living in poverty, whatever her income percentage may be.

Those who scan the horizon for injustices have a field day with the statistics generated by these social patterns. Villains and maidens in distress have always been good melodrama. The media eat it up. So do political crusaders.

One of the great hoaxes of our time is that "women's liberation" has brought great improvements in the representation of women in higher occupations. In reality, women were better represented in many high-level fields half a century ago than today. Back in the 1930s, women received a far higher percentage of the doctoral degrees in mathematics, chemistry, economics and law than in the 1960s. They were far better represented in professional careers in 1940 than 25 years later. What has happened between the 1930s and today was (1) the baby boom and (2) the end of the baby boom.

Just as motherhood is crucial for understanding the economic situation of women at a given time, so it is crucial for understanding what has happened over time. As women began having more babies, they began having fewer high-level careers. When the birth rates began to fall in the 1960s, women's representation rose in many high-level fields.

In some fields, it is still not back to where it was two generations ago. In other fields it is. In a few fields, it is higher. In all fields, "women's liberation" takes the credit.

This is only one of many areas in which political crusaders promote their bogeyman explanations of economic differences. The real puzzle is why they are so seldom questioned, much less challenged.

—April 25, 1984

Cutting the Budget

If there is going to be any hope of significantly cutting federal spending, we are first going to have to cut through a lot of foggy thinking.

Politics being what it is, no one should be surprised that Chicken Littles are running around yelling that the sky is falling, because their part of the federal budget may be reduced. What is sad is how many others take them seriously.

The confusion spreads right across the political spectrum—from the mushiest liberal to the most stern and rockbound conservative. Liberal Tom Wicker of the *New York Times* wants the government to keep subsidizing the Amtrak railroad. George Will, America's foremost conservative journalist, wants the government to keep subsidizing farmers.

Even the usually intelligent *Wall Street Journal* ran a story asking us to share the anguish of a $40,000-a-year man who might lose a few federal goodies.

According to the *Wall St. Journal* story, there will be a "pervasive" effect of budget cuts on the middle class. For starters, elimination of federal subsidies to public utilities could cause their $40,000-a-year man's electricity bills to rise "by $50 or more"—per year.

That's about a dollar a week.

If we are going to start worrying about whether some guy who makes 40 grand can pay a buck a week more for electricity, we may as well give up all pretense of reducing the federal deficit. There's no way to reduce the government's outflow of money without reducing someone's inflow.

Why should a newborn baby enter the world owing money on the national debt for this fellow's electric bill? If we don't understand that every government giveaway is a take-away from somebody else, we can end up falling for every sob story that comes along.

If we had to go into the red to save the hungry and the destitute, that would be one thing. But if the hungry and the destitute were the only ones getting government handouts, we could balance the budget tomorrow.

It's not even a question of national belt-tightening to reduce the deficit. Right now there are people whose belts are tighter than they have to be, because politicians are directing resources away from them, toward others with more political clout. As a nation, we don't make any magical gains by subsidizing each other. Insofar as subsidies encourage waste and inefficiency, we have less.

George Will proves that conservatives can ignore this as completely as liberals. Will has argued that farm subsidies are justified because agriculture has been beneficial.

One of the grand fallacies of our time is that something beneficial should be subsidized. But it is precisely by *not* subsidizing it that we find out whether its benefits cover its costs—and limit it to the amount that is still beneficial.

An abundance of food is certainly a national benefit, but only up to a point. When the agricultural surplus starts taking up massive amounts of costly space in warehouses and in the federal budget, it has gone way past the point of being beneficial.

Agricultural subsidies cost the government $22 billion a year. The farms receiving these subsidies have average assets of more than one million dollars each. True, many of these assets have been mortgaged, on the gamble that still more surplus food could be absorbed by the market or by the government. But why should the taxpayers' money be used to turn every gamble into a guarantee?

Even more ridiculous arguments are used to justify pouring money down a bottomless pit to subsidize the Amtrak railroad. Not even someone as liberal as Tom

Wicker can claim that the hungry and the destitute are commuting on Amtrak.

Nor is it the case that the public won't be able to go where they want to without Amtrak. Anywhere a train can go, a bus can usually go more cheaply and an airplane can go faster. That is the very reason why Amtrak cannot pay its own way—and why the taxpayers shouldn't.

Wicker says that Amtrak provides "a needed choice of inter-city transportation modes." When they start talking like bureaucrats, you know the case won't stand up in plain English.

Sure, there are people who would rather ride the railroad, and they should be free to have their druthers, as we say in North Carolina. They should also pay for it, so the taxpayers can likewise be free to have their druthers.

Finally, Wicker warns that if the government sells Amtrak, to a private railroad, the United States will become one of the few nations "lacking a national rail passenger service." We are also one of the very few countries with a privately owned telephone system. It is far more efficient than most government-owned systems. What a coincidence!

—February 21, 1985

Who Are "the Poor"?

Upon hearing that a New Yorker is hit by a car once every 20 minutes, the listener replied: "Gee, he must get awfully tired of that."

Bad logic like this may be all right for jokes. But such reasoning has also become commonplace when deep thinkers start talking about social policy.

We hear so much about "the poor," "the unemployed," "the homeless." But the poor are not a class of people doomed to a certain fate.

Just as it is not the same New Yorker who gets hit by a car every 20 minutes, it is not the same people who fall into the "poor" bracket every year. Nearly half the people who are poor one year are out of the poverty bracket the following year. Many get out in a few months.

The unemployed, the homeless, and people on welfare also have considerable turnover. Misfortunes strike people, but most of them don't just lie there.

The statistics we hear thrown around by deep thinkers and moralizers do not represent permanent classes of people. Being poor is not like being left-handed or brown-eyed. You are not that way for life.

Nothing is set in concrete—especially not in the United States. This is true of the upper income brackets as well. Half the people in the top 20 percent of income earners one year are not there just a few years later. And most of their adult offspring are not in the top 20 percent.

Many of the income differences that our deep thinkers wring their hands about are connected with age. Young people who are just starting to work don't usually earn nearly as much as people with 20 years of experience behind them.

Income differences between the middle-aged and the young are greater than income differences between blacks and whites. It's just that no one notices these differences.

The constant cries about income inequalities, disparities, and "inequities" ignore great differences among the people involved. A young fellow in his twenties may be making half the income of his father. But is that an injustice?

Do we need a government program to rush to the aid of this young man—who will almost inevitably be an older man someday? He may already be able to afford some luxuries that his father cannot afford, because his father has heavier responsibilities—like putting kids through college or preparing for his own retirement.

Deep thinkers don't want to be distracted by these kinds of details. To them the big thing is that the numbers don't look equal on paper.

This gives them an opportunity to strike moral poses and denounce American society. The grubby details they leave to others.

The media adds to the confusion. It can always find someone to put on television to represent "the poor." The more heart-rending the predicament, the better for TV ratings. Truth and balance are lost in the shuffle.

Reckless crusades are the lifeblood of journalism. Anthony Trollope wrote a novel about it more than a hundred years ago, so it's not a new thing.

What is new is that television gives a sense of immediacy and reality to half-baked notions, and brings it all into millions of homes every night under the label of "news."

True poverty, homelessness and hunger are painful. I can assure you of that from personal experience.

But the answer is not to sanctify poverty or to denounce those who have stayed out of poverty. Poverty is not to be made a career—either for those who are in it or those who administer programs for the poor.

The answer to poverty is prosperity—not being maudlin to those who fall into the category of "the poor" at a given moment. The welfare state and the taxes required to support it stifle the very creation of jobs that are needed to provide opportunities to escape poverty.

European welfare states have gone much further than the United States. Recently Europeans have begun to express surprise that they are not nearly as successful at creating jobs as those "heartless" Americans. Maybe some of our own deep thinkers ought to take notice.

The only way the government can create jobs is by taking resources from the private sector. That means fewer jobs in the private sector.

That is no answer to unemployment. All it does is let politicians look like benefactors, when in fact they are making things worse.

—December 30, 1984

Lessons from Coca-Cola

The recent tempest in a teapot over the changing flavor of Coca-Cola has lessons that go well beyond soft drinks.

Several years of market research went into the decision to change the flavor of this drink that has been around for nearly a century. The same kind of terribly clever survey researchers who advise judges, legislators, government agencies, and the media, told Coca-Cola that the new flavor would be more popular than the old. The company bought it. The customers didn't.

All sorts of things started happening—very quickly. Sales began falling. Coke dealers started complaining to the company. Speculators rushed in to buy up the old-flavored version wherever they could find it. Panic hit the corporate headquarters.

The net result was that—in a matter of weeks—one of the business giants of America did a complete flip-flop. The old flavor came back and the new flavor remained as well. This meant suddenly scrapping more than four years of planning for the changeover in flavors.

Although the company suffered some public embarrassment, sales went back up—and sales are where it's at. Coca-Cola management will no doubt be happy to settle for being number one in their industry, even if their marketing fiasco lives on for years in the case studies at business schools.

There are a number of lessons in all this. Deep thinkers have been telling us for years that big business so "dominates" our economy that their mass advertising can make consumers buy whatever the big corporations market. No big corporation is fool enough to believe that—certainly not when sales are falling. But opinion-makers in the media and academe often accept it as gospel.

Those who take survey researchers in deadly seriousness in other areas need to have some second thoughts— or perhaps it will be the first thoughts for some. Charts, graphs, and computer printouts can be very impressive, but so were the old-time snake oil salesmen. Gimmicks do not make thinking or experience obsolete.

The biggest lesson of all is that the economic marketplace forces even the most clever ideas to surrender unconditionally to reality. Neither judges, legislators, bureaucrats, nor media deep thinkers have to admit to being wrong so quickly or change courses so decisively.

Everyone from the "mom and pop" store on the corner to the biggest corporation on Wall Street has to shape up or ship out. Big-time speculators, frantically shouting out their bids and offers on the floor of the exchanges, are often correcting their mistakes on things that looked good just a little while ago. A local commodity speculator in the town of Palo Alto says that he has lost $100,000 in a day, and the big corporate speculators can lose millions in a few hours. The multi-billionaire Hunt brothers in Texas lost so many millions speculating in silver that they required huge loans from the banks to keep afloat.

The greatness of a competitive economy is that it forces

constant revisions of our estimates and changes in our behavior when we are mistaken. If we were omniscient, there would be no point in free enterprise or a competitive economy. Appointed officials could issue orders from on high to do the right thing, and that would be the end of it.

Tragically, many people act as if that is the way we can operate right now. Deep thinkers are constantly urging judges, politicians, or bureaucrats to impose some pet idea on other people—"pay equity," "social justice," or a thousand other high-sounding notions. It never seems to occur to them that even wonderfully brilliant and soulfully compassionate people like themselves could be wrong.

The issue is not which policy has the most ringing sound but what institutions have the fastest and most thorough corrections if they turn out to be wrong. It certainly is not the federal judiciary appointed for life or civil servants or professors with tenure.

—July 22, 1985

Incentives

One of the remarkable things about the Chinese is how they prosper in a wide range of societies around the world—but not in China.

One of the key ingredients in the success of the Chinese is their indefatigable capacity for work. Whether as plantation laborers in colonial Malaya, storekeepers from Thailand to Jamaica, or engineering students from Cal Tech to M.I.T., the Chinese are noted for long hours of painstaking work.

Against this background, it is especially striking to encounter a recent story out of Communist China about the problems of trying to get workers there to do a decent day's work. American Motors has a plant in China to manufacture Jeeps. But the assembly line workers are a study in slow motion—and sometimes no motion. One worker, after reading his newspaper, simply sat down on a bench and fell asleep. A photographer for the *New York Times* captured him on film for posterity.

The Chinese goofing off? American college professors and students may find it hard to believe. Anyone who has seen the frenzied work ethic in such overseas Chinese communities as Hong Kong or Singapore will find it almost inconceivable. Yet statistics show that it takes the average auto worker in American Motors' Beijing plant more than two weeks to do the same amount of work that an American auto worker does in less than one week in the company's Toldeo plant.

Auto making is not an unusual case. People in Hong Kong report that in general refugees from Communist China often make very unproductive workers until enough time passes for them to get into the Hong Kong spirit. The problem is very simple: incentives.

In an economic system in China that offers relatively little to hope for in material rewards and relatively little to fear, such as unemployment, there are often not enough incentives to do your best. Once refugees from China get reoriented to the fact that their income can vary considerably in Hong Kong, according to their own efforts, those efforts increase.

Even in countries where the Chinese encountered harsh discrimination, which restricted their occupations, they could nevertheless make more money by working hard than by taking it easy. It was not justice but incentives that were economically crucial.

The Chinese are not unique in their widely differing

responses to different incentives. There are levels of inefficiency in Israel which are hard to believe for anyone familiar with Jewish communities in other countries. Israel too has a suffocating set of economic policies along socialistic lines.

If the wrong incentives can undermine the efficiency of the Chinese and the Jews, they can undermine anybody. It is not a racial issue but a human issue.

Recent attention to the tragic situation of many black families too often makes it appear as a racial matter, simply because they compare blacks and whites, or blacks and the "national average." Actually, similar levels of teenage pregnancy and female-headed families have existed for years among Puerto Ricans.

But welfare state benefits are not very tempting to groups with better economic prospects. Teenage girls who have good prospects of going on to college, and perhaps postgraduate education, have too much at stake to throw it all away and end up as welfare mothers. Black girls who are on a different track in life also have very different child-bearing patterns. Black teenagers who are married have fewer children than white teenagers who are married—and both have fewer children than welfare mothers.

The Soviet Union's housing incentives often cause an even more tragic family fragmentation than here, according to Dr. Mikhail Bernstam of the Hoover Institution. Young women new to a big city like Moscow or Leningrad may face a very bleak prospect of waiting for an apartment—unless they have a child, which moves them up on the waiting list. Many get pregnant, get the apartment, and then put the baby in an orphanage. Now, as a young woman with her own apartment, she is very eligible for marriage.

In country after country, too many social programs are discussed in terms of the wonderful goals they are meant to achieve. Much more attention needs to be paid to the incentives created and their actual consequences.

Human beings around the world seem to respond to incentives more so than to rhetoric.

—April 14, 1985

Social Security: A Fraudulent Pyramid Club

Social Security is the longest-running fraud in America. At no time in its history has there been enough money in the till to pay out all the benefits that the politicians wrote into the law.

Now the truth is catching up with them. The funds have dropped so low that the Social Security Administration can't even keep up appearances much longer by taking from the young to pay off the old. If nothing is done, Social Security will run out of money in 1982.

Ironically, President Reagan is catching hell for being the messenger bearing the bad news. His attempt to rescue the system at the 11th hour has unleashed charges of heartlessness and claims that the government is defaulting on its promise to the American people. But that promise was a fraud from the beginning. Long before Reagan arrived in Washington, many of those who are now yelling the loudest—Rep. Claude Pepper (D-Fla.), for example—

were promising benefits that could not be paid out of the premiums.

Social Security insiders have known for decades that they were selling the public a bill of goods under the guise of "insurance."

But even some staunch Social Security advocates long ago admitted that it was no such thing. When an insurance company writes a policy, it has to have enough assets to pay out what it promises. Otherwise the company can be declared bankrupt and its officials can go to jail. Any insurance company that had the same benefits, premiums and reserves as the Social Security system would be shut down by court order and its managers led away in handcuffs to face charges of fraud.

If Social Security is not insurance, what is it? It is much like a pyramid club, where the members who join first get paid out of what is collected from the members who join later. That works fine as long as there are more new members than old members. But eventually somebody gets left holding the empty bag. That is where we are today with Social Security.

When the population was growing rapidly, there were more young workers than retired workers, so the Social Security pyramid scheme worked. Now that there are proportionately fewer young people than old people, the federal pyramid scheme is about to collapse. Just as some people get angry when the police stop pyramid clubs before the members collect the money that they expected, so some people are angry at the Reagan Administration for interfering with the benefits that they were promised. And, as in pyramid schemes, there is no way for all the members to get all the benefits that they expect.

Private insurance companies invest each person's premiums so that there will be enough money accumulated to pay off the policies—regardless of how many members join. But, in the case of Social Security, today's incoming checks are being used to cover today's outgoing checks. The reserves are so low that Social Security checks will start bouncing in 1982 unless something is done.

Something will be done, of course. The question is what. But the larger question is, why do we continue to allow politicians to write laws promising benefits that they have not raised money to pay for?

Rep. Jim Wright (D-Tex.) says that the Social Security system can be made "actuarially sound" without cutting benefits. But to be actuarially sound it must have enough assets to cover its liabilities, and Social Security will not be actuarially sound even if all the Reagan Administration's proposed cutbacks are enacted. All that the Administration's plan will do is prevent Social Security checks from bouncing and let the current generation of elderly people relax. Actuaries estimate that the system will be on the verge of bankruptcy again in the early twenty-first century. It is still a pyramid scheme.

A move is afoot to enact a constitutional amendment requiring that the budget be balanced. The same principle should apply to pension plans. The premiums collected should provide a large enough reserve to offset what the plan has promised to pay out. Social Security and many pension plans for municipal, state and federal employees do not do that. They offer a better deal than private pension plans precisely because they do not have to have the money to back up their promises.

As long as we keep expecting politicians to give us something for nothing, we should also continue to expect financial crises—not only in Social Security but up and down the line as well.

—July 3, 1981

Authorized Lying

The truth and the public are both great inconveniences to politicians in power. Treasury Secretary Donald Regan now proposes that banks be officially authorized to lie to the public about the bad loans they made to Third World countries.

The banks are already lying unofficially. Bank reports include in their earnings interest they "expect" to receive from loans to Third World countries. Argentina hasn't made any such payments in months. Yet bank reports keep listing Argentine payments that they "expect," just as if they had actually received them.

It makes bank earnings look good on paper. Nobody is fooled but the public. Argentina hasn't even said, "The check is in the mail." Nobody in his right mind expects Argentina—or many other Third World debtors—to pay off their debts, or even to keep up the interest payments.

The only real issue is whether the bankers and the politicians can keep on fooling the public. After 90 days of not even receiving interest payments, the law requires banks to stop listing phantom "expected" payments among their earnings reported to the public. Secretary Regan thinks these bank regulations should be "relaxed."

So what if Argentina's payments are $650 million overdue? It could happen to anyone. In fact, Mexico, Brazil, and many other Third World countries have also run up whopping debts, on which they may or may not be able to make interest payments.

All this international crisis atmosphere is over interest payments only. No one is Utopian enough to expect that the principal will be repaid—unless the American taxpayers pay it.

There are all sorts of high-sounding words to conceal

these plain facts from the public. Loans are "rescheduled." That means that if they don't pay now, we will postpone their payments till later. And when later comes, we can postpone them again.

Then there are "adjustment" loans. That means you give them new loans to pay off their old loans. That means that loans are not repaid, just rolled over.

This not only makes bankers look good on paper, it does the same for government agencies that pour the taxpayers' money down a bottomless pit to subsidize shaky governments in chaotic countries. As long as loans are rolled over, the books don't show what huge losses are being suffered by the taxpayers, bank depositors and stockholders.

"A rolling loan gathers no loss," is the way one banker put it. An audience of bankers roared with laughter at hearing it phrased that way. Whether the American taxpayers would be as amused, if they understood, is another question entirely.

Treasury Secretary Regan has urged "strengthening" the "resources" of the International Monetary Fund, which deals with financial problems among nations. That sounds good. Most things politicians say sound good. That's why you have to look at the fine print.

In plain English, the "strengthening" of I.M.F. "resources" means spending more American dollars to prop up irresponsible big spenders in the Third World. We are not talking about keeping starving people alive. There are relief agencies for doing that. We are talking about picking up the tab for showy new subway systems, government buildings and whole new capital cities built in Third World countries with borrowed money.

We are talking about letting them go on doing more of the same, without paying off what they owe already. When Federal Reserve Chairman Paul Volcker talks about "continuing credit to maintain continuity of payments," that means giving them more money just so they can pay the interest on what they already owe. A high official of one of the big banks being rescued by government bailout activity speaks fondly of "a remarkable degree of coordination" among government officials and commercial lenders. He says, "The process is working." It is working for him—but not for the taxpayers.

All this roundabout language fools no one but the public. If they ever catch on, the party's over.

—April 9, 1984

The Economics of Language

T he controversies surrounding so-called "bilingual" education have produced all kinds of moralistic, psychological, and political rhetoric. But they have seldom been examined economically. How much is it worth to speak English?

That is what the issue comes down to, for "bilingual" education seldom involves actually learning two languages. Usually it means teaching children in their native language, with pious hopes that they will eventually learn English. How much economic difference does it make if they don't?

American Indians are one of the few groups that make lower family incomes than blacks. Yet American Indian males who grow up in homes where English was the language spoken earn as much as white males who are similar in other characteristics. So do Hispanic males. Hispanics who grew up in English-speaking homes finished high school about 50 percent more often than those who grew up in Spanish-speaking homes—and finished college 70 percent more often.

No doubt language alone is not responsible for all these economic and educational differences. The kind of people who take the trouble to learn the language of the surrounding society, and to see that their children learn it from an early age, probably have different attitudes and priorities in general. That is also relevant to the "bilingual" controversy. For language is only part of a more general effort to keep children in a separate culture. Whether the economic damage suffered by this approach is due solely to language or to the other insulating features of bilingualism is a secondary question. The children lose out either way.

These economic facts of life carry little weight in politics, especially during an election year. The name of the game is appeasing vocal political activists and hustlers, for whom bilingualism provides jobs, grants, and a segregated constituency that needs them. Making children fluent in English means preparing them to be self-reliant adults. But while self-reliant people who can function on their own in the larger society may make more money, they are no longer a captive audience for ethnic "leaders."

The economic effect of teaching "Black English" in the schools is very similar to that of teaching Spanish or other, more widely recognized, languages. It insulates, reduces communication and promotes provincialism. It also produces a captive audience for "leaders."

The economic value of language depends on what kinds of work are performed. Most first-generation Japanese immigrants to the United States spoke only broken English or no English at all. Yet they rose up the ladder as self-employed farmers or businessmen.

Other groups in other countries had similar experiences—as long as they could be self-employed, or employed predominantly by other members of their own group. There were German enclaves in czarist Russia where there was little need to speak Russian, and where some of the children had never seen a Russian. But they were largely self-employed farmers or businessmen who served their own communities. There have been similar Japanese enclaves in Brazil or Chinese enclaves in Southeast Asia.

It is when you are employed by other people, or in businesses that deal with the larger society, that language becomes a matter of economic life and death. Blacks, Hispanics, and American Indians are generally in no economic position to hire each other. Even groups that begin in their own enclaves, and prosper there, eventually reach the point where their further progress requires knowing the language and culture of the society around them. Most Japanese Americans today grow up speaking English, go on to college—and earn more than white Americans. A Japanese farmer out in California's fertile valleys did not need to speak much English in order to sell his vegetables, but his son the engineer does have to be able to communicate with other engineers.

One of the few encouraging signs about American education is that youngsters from groups that have long been behind are beginning to reduce the educational gap. The difference between the College Board scores of blacks and whites was reduced on both the verbal and quantitative tests between 1977 and 1982. This was due primarily to a rise in the scores of blacks, but the scores of whites also declined somewhat over the same span. The scores of Mexican Americans also rose slightly.

These improvements need to be encouraged. Mastery of English and math are not mere accommodations to chauvinism in the dominant culture. They are what enable the individual to draw upon the knowledge and analysis of the whole human race, in this and previous ages. Illiteracy in words or numbers is too heavy a handicap to put on any group, whatever its self-appointed "leaders" or "spokesmen" may say.

—June 17, 1984

Oil Prices

The true mark of a deep thinker is that, no matter how wrong the facts prove him to be, he is utterly self-confident with his next assertion. "Often wrong but never in doubt" should be his motto.

The "oil crisis" of the 1970s brought the deep thinkers out of the woodwork everywhere. To them it proved—as everything always does—the need for the government to control our lives, as the only way to avoid total disaster. When a few people like Milton Friedman bucked the tide and said that government controls were the cause of the crisis, and that decontrol was the cure, they were howled down.

When Ronald Reagan said that decontrol and the normal operation of the marketplace would bring down oil prices and relieve the shortage, to deep thinkers it only showed how "simplistic" he was. They turned their deadliest weapon on him: sneer power.

When gasoline prices recently began dropping below one dollar a gallon, it was a big surprise to the deep thinkers and big news in the media. No one seemed to remember that this was the very opposite of widespread predictions that gasoline prices would rise to over two dollars a gallon. However, the current issue of *Policy Review* magazine has published a large collection of quotes from those who made such predictions. It should be required reading.

Senators Ted Kennedy and Howard Metzenbaum and Congressman John Dingell all predicted that gasoline prices would go over two dollars a gallon. So did Nobel Prize-winning economist Kenneth Arrow. So did Lester Brown of World Watch Institute, writing in the prestigious *Bulletin of the Atomic Scientists* and the equally prestigious *Foreign Affairs* quarterly. Oil expert Dan Lundberg had similarly pessimistic predictions. Senator Dale Bumpers predicted gasoline prices of three dollars a gallon. Sheik Yamani of OPEC predicted even higher prices.

Predictions of declining oil production, rising prices, national "emergency" and "world depression" were commonplace. Among those contributing to such hysteria were *Business Week* magazine, *New York Times* economic writer Leonard Silk, as well as various officials of the Carter Administration. President Carter himself said that oil prices "are going to rise in the future no matter who is President, no matter which party occupies the administration in Washington, no matter what we do."

As usual, all this hysteria was not without some political purpose. The bottom line was more government power. Ted Kennedy advocated "gasoline rationing without delay" and urged his fellow Democrats to oppose decontrol. His fellow Massachusetts Democrats Congressmen Markey and Mavroules joined the chants. The former said, "Decontrol as a cure will prove to be worse than the disease of oil addiction." The latter predicted that heating oil prices would rise so high that the average Massachusetts household would be paying more for fuel than their total taxes. (Heating costs have in fact gone down.)

Mere government controls were not enough for Glyn

Jones, who said in the *New York Times:* "America's oil system must be *nationalized* as are those of Libya, Nigeria, Mexico, and Venezuela." Except for Libya, these are countries the deep thinkers are now asking us to bail out with the American taxpayers' money, because oil prices have fallen.

Needless to say, the fall in oil prices now proves to deep thinkers once again that the government must step in to avert disaster. The Democrats have no monopoly on this fallacy. Vice-President George Bush has made hysterical statements worthy of Ted Kennedy, including his incredible suggestion that we encourage OPEC to keep oil prices from falling.

No matter how many times the marketplace works and government controls fail, deep thinkers are going to prefer government controls. Controlling the economy sounds so logical, so humane, so right. And how it sounds is what matters to politicians—and to too many intellectuals.

Wherever the government sets prices below the market level, shortages are virtually guaranteed. It may take the form of gasoline lines, as it did in the 1970s here, food lines as in Eastern Europe, waiting lists for automobiles in India, or interminable searches for apartments in cities with rent control—whether in America, Europe or Asia. Government-imposed prices created shortages under the Emperor Diocletian in the days of the Roman Empire. Prices imposed to make food "affordable" to the masses created widespread hunger instead when the French did it in the 1790s, when the Russians did it after the Bolshevik Revolution, and in numerous African countries in our own time.

At some point we have to start paying attention to results rather than rhetoric.

—July 14, 1986

"Comparable Worth" Rides Again

The Chairman of the U.S. Commission on Civil Rights has called comparable worth "the looniest idea since Looney Tunes."

True believers were outraged. But my only objection is to the injustice done to Looney Tunes, which had some classic and hilarious cartoons. Comparable worth is equally ridiculous, but not nearly as funny.

Comparable worth or "pay equity" is not just an American phenomenon. Recently, in Britain, it was ruled that a woman working in a shipyard's canteen was of equivalent value to a male carpenter on an oil rig out in the Irish Sea. A distinguished British economist who read the report on which this decision was based said: "I wonder how all this can be taken seriously by anybody who is not paid a fee to keep a straight face when reading it." Comparable worth is an idea whose time has come—and whose logic has gone.

If we buy the key assumption of comparable worth—that third party observers can tell what jobs are "really" worth—then our whole economic system should be scrapped. Why let supply and demand determine wages—or product prices, or interest rates, or anything else—if you can tell what things are "really" worth and establish that equitably?

If somebody has this God-like ability, why restrict it to cases involving jobs that are predominantly male or female? Aren't we all entitled to "pay equity"? And why not rent equity, tuition equity, vacation equity, and all kinds of other equity?

Supply and demand is why not. Employers do not choose salaries in a seminar. They pay what they have to pay, in

116

the competition of the labor market, to get the job done—and usually not a dollar more, if they can help it. People who go around saying that women are paid only 59 percent of what men get are in effect saying that employers could cut their labor costs 41 percent, just by hiring women instead of men. If that were true, there wouldn't be an unemployed woman in America—or an employed man.

It is of course not true. A closer look at the statistics shows that the famous "59 percent" is gotten by comparing apples and oranges—women who work hundreds of hours less than men annually, for example.

People who spend their lives dealing with words easily overlook the fact that other people have to base their decisions on something more concrete. If an employer finds that he cannot get enough carpenters for what he is paying, he is going to have to raise the pay of carpenters. And if he can easily get more people to work in the canteen, he is not going to raise the pay there.

If people are more willing to work in a canteen on shore than on an oil rig at sea, then pay differences will reflect that fact, whether the workers are men or women. So-called "experts" cannot tell these people they are wrong. Each individual is the biggest expert on what he or she wants.

Many predominantly male jobs have requirements that are especially difficult for women. Physical strength is only one of many reasons. How many pregnant women want to be working out in the middle of nowhere when time comes to go to the maternity ward? Even among single women graduating from college or getting a Ph.D., their fields of specialization are drastically different from those of men.

Once we admit that we are neither God nor Superman, it becomes easier to admit that we cannot possibly know all the reasons for all the individual preferences and decisions summarized as supply and demand. Neither does the employer. All he knows is that he can fill certain jobs more easily than others.

The comparable worth principle is the principle that kibitzers know best. At its worst, it is the principle that employers are guilty until proven innocent. It is a guarantee of full employment for lawyers, consultants and activists. As long as the courts are willing to award people hard cash for high-sounding words, you may be sure that there will be a flood of such words, an army of litigants, and a clogged court system.

But that is only the tip of the iceberg. An economy gummed up by wages and prices that no longer reflect supply and demand is not the kind of economy that produced the American standard of living. Looney Tunes? No, Mr. Chairman, comparable worth isn't funny at all.

—June 18, 1985

Reagan's Economic Policies

"**M**r. President, all Washington was shocked today when the administration introduced legislation to end agricultural price support subsidies. Can you explain the reason for this drastic move?"

"Well, it's no more drastic than cutting food stamps or school lunches. You can't very well go around saying that we're in an economic emergency requiring painful cutbacks in bloated government, and still keep pouring billions of dollars of tax money into the coffers of farm owners and huge agricultural corporations."

"Mr. President, if I may follow up on the other reporter's question: does this mean an end to dairy price supports as well?"

"Yes. A lot of the fat in government is butterfat."

"Excuse me, Mr. President, but won't there be political hell to pay among your supporters? What will Sen. Dole say when you cut off all that federal money to Kansas wheat farmers? Won't Sen. Helms be mad when you end subsidies to tobacco farmers in North Carolina?"

"Well, a handout's a handout, no matter who gets it. When we're trying to get people off welfare, we can't keep Kansas farmers on the dole. (No pun intended.) As for tobacco, I thought that was hazardous to your health."

"How far are you prepared to carry this, Mr. President? Would you deny federal disaster aid to people whose homes slid down the hillsides during the recent California rains?"

"Much of that disaster occurred in some of the most affluent areas in the country. When you build a mansion on top of an unstable hill, how can you expect the average taxpayer to help you put it back up there after it's slid down?"

"But federal rebuilding loans are not a handout, sir. The recipients have to repay them with interest."

"But how much interest? If the federal government borrows money at 17 percent and lends it at 7 percent, that's the same as giving away 10 percent of the loan."

"I suppose you could look at it that way, Mr. President, but . . ."

"Let me finish. Now, when somebody rebuilds a half-million-dollar mansion in Marin county, a loan subsidy of 10 percentage points is $50,000 a year. Why should the ordinary taxpayer be giving that kind of money every year to somebody who can afford a half-million-dollar mansion?"

"Mr. President, would you also stop aiding the automobile companies?"

"You mean the Chrysler bailout? Yes. If the marketplace says it's a lemon, there's no reason for the U.S. Treasury to say it's a peach."

"Well, I wasn't just thinking of Chrysler. What about your administration's pressure on Japan to stop sending so many cars here?"

"That policy's being changed, too. I just told the Japanese ambassador, 'The more the merrier.' "

"That's a stunning reversal of policy, Mr. President. Won't that have a disastrous effect on our automobile companies?"

"Why should the ordinary citizen be compelled to subsidize the automobile companies? If he can save hundreds of dollars by buying an import, that's his right."

"Have you no compassion for the automobile company stockholders and workers?"

"They have their own safety nets. An automobile worker who loses his job gets so many benefits that he will have more money coming in when he is unemployed than millions of other Americans get for working full-time."

"And what about the stockholders, Mr. President?"

"Stockholders get paid for taking risks. That's why stocks earn more than insured savings accounts."

"You would cut them off without a cent of federal aid?"

"The private sector can take up the slack."

"How, Mr. President?"

"Lots of ways. In the good old American tradition, their friends and neighbors could pass the hat at the local country club. Nieman-Marcus or Lord & Taylor might give them a special discount. There are lots of ways, without always relying on government."

"But is it right, Mr. President, to single out stockholders for special sacrifice, while the government is still spending billions on the sick and the poor?"

"Well, we've already cut CETA and housing subsidies, and we're getting ready to cut Medicare and Social Security. So we are spreading the sacrifice around. After all, I am president of all the people."

"Ronnie! Ronnie!"

"Who's calling me, 'Ronnie'?"

"It's me, Ronnie! Wake Up!"

"Oh, Nancy. My God! I just had a nightmare. Reporters were asking the damndest questions—and I was giving the damndest answers."

—January 26, 1982,
© *Washington Post*

IV

POLITICS

A Political Glossary

Every field has its own special words and expressions, which others find hard to understand. Politics is no exception. For those who have difficulty understanding the strange way words are used by politicians and the media, here is a glossary translating political rhetoric into plain English:

"crisis": any situation you want to change

"bilingual": unable to speak English

"equal opportunity": preferential treatment

"non-judgmental": blaming society

"compassion": the use of tax money to buy votes

"insensitivity": objections to the use of tax money to buy votes

"simplistic": an argument you disagree with but can't answer

"rehabilitation": magic word said before releasing criminals

"demonstration": a riot by people you agree with

"mob violence": a riot by people you disagree with

"a matter of principle": a political controversy involving the convictions of liberals

"an emotional issue": a political controversy involving the convictions of conservatives

"funding": money from the government

"commitment": more money from the government

"docu-drama": a work of fiction about famous people

"autobiography": a work of fiction about yourself

"federal budget": a work of fiction about government spending

"people's republic": a place where you do what you are told or get shot

"national liberation movements": organizations trying to create people's republics

"policy research": looking for statistics to support the position you have already taken

"stereotypes": behavior patterns you don't want to think about

"Reaganomics": media explanation of downturns in the economy

"robust economy": media explanation of upturns in the economy

"constitutional interpretation": judges reading their own political views into the Constitution

"politicizing the courts": criticizing judges for reading their own political views into the Constitution

"a proud people": chauvinists you like

"bigots": chauvinists you don't like

"anti-war movement": disarmament advocates who know the idea won't fly under its own name

"private greed": making money selling people what they want

"public service": gaining power to make people do what you want them to

"innovation": something new

"new innovation": something new by someone who doesn't understand English

"competency": competence, as described by the incompetent

"moderate Arabs": mythical beings to whom State Department officials make sacrificial offerings

"special interest lobby": politically organized conservatives

"public interest group": politically organized liberals

"accountability": holding teachers, public officials, and private businesses responsible for the consequences of their misdeeds

"chilling effect": holding journalists responsible for the consequences of their misdeeds

—November 8, 1985

Left versus Right

One of the basic problems of conservatives was illustrated by an industrialist in his 70s who was bitterly complaining about a liberal Senator from his state—a Senator who seemed almost certain to be re-elected.

"If I were twenty years younger," the conservative industrialist said, "I would run against him myself!"

Maybe. But there was a time when he was 20 years younger—and he didn't run against any liberals then.

When bright, educated young people are choosing careers, those who believe in a free market economy often choose careers in that economy. Those opposed to such an economy are more likely to become intellectuals, politicians, lawyers, or parts of various liberal or radical movements.

For the intellectual and political battles, the deck is stacked, both quantitatively and qualitatively. The political left sends its A team into battle against the B team of its critics, who have their A team in the marketplace.

The historic drift to the left in the Western world over the generations reflects in good part this imbalance in the world of ideas, rather than any success of left-wing politics when actually put into practice. Such policies have a record of economic disaster around the world, especially in Communist countries, but they are a roaring success politically in maintaining the support of academic and media intellectuals.

All that has prevented the total and conclusive victory of the political left are the defections from its own ranks—people who have been following the facts and have become fed up with what they have seen. Most of the leading figures who oppose the liberals and leftists in the United States are former liberals and leftists.

Ronald Reagan and Milton Friedman were both liberals at one time. As a member of the liberal-left Americans for Democratic Action, Reagan called Barry Goldwater a "fascist." Friedman had a hand in drafting some of the New Deal legislation he now bitterly attacks.

Irving Kristol, the godfather of neo-conservatism, was once a Marxist. Such other leading neo-conservatives as Nathan Glazer and Norman Podhoretz were once prominent supporters of liberal causes.

Among blacks today regarded as "conservative," virtually all were once either liberals or leftists. Harvard professor Glenn Loury, who has criticized preferential treatment programs in recent years, was defending such programs earlier in this decade. Walter Williams was such a vocal radical, while serving as a young draftee in the U.S. Army, that he was court-martialed.

This pattern of young liberals and radicals turning against these doctrines as they mature is not confined to the United States or to our own era. It may simply reflect the fact that the case for the political left looks more plausible on the surface but is harder to keep believing in as you become more experienced.

So many middle-aged conservatives are former young liberals and radicals that many of them find it hard to understand young conservatives, libertarians, and other youthful opponents of the left. Their suspicion may be based on the old cliché: "If you're not radical in your twenties, you have no heart—and if you are still radical in your forties, you have no head."

But some of the young libertarians and conservatives I have seen don't strike me as heartless at all. Many are deeply concerned about the tragic social consequences of high-sounding liberal-left programs. Some of the highest quality thinking and writing among college students today is found in campus newspapers like the *Harvard Salient,* the *California Review,* and other student papers that stand up to the dominant leftism among the "official" student newspapers and among the faculty.

These youngsters have no choice but to think, because they cannot get by with simply chanting slogans about "social justice," "divestment," and "world peace," as the political left does.

The left does not have to think on campus, just chant and demonstrate and feel morally superior. They can win by intimidation on campus, given the favoritism of the faculty and the pliability of the administration. As a result, they are now becoming intellectually the B team.

—September 25, 1986

Government Careers

In the Fiji islands a couple of years ago, the sight of Fijians in their native costumes, dancing barefoot on red-hot coals, reminded me of nominees at Senate confirmation hearings.

Ordeals for those seeking public office have increased greatly over the years. Disclosures of your personal life in minute detail are now an accepted fact of life. So are public humiliations handed out at confirmation hearings to people whose only crime is to have different political opinions from those of Senators on the confirmation committee.

Any criticisms of these savage rites of passage are sure to be met with some such comment as: "If you can't take it, you don't belong in politics." Like many pieces of rhetoric suggesting hard-headed "practicality," it is not only impractical but downright silly, because it addresses a completely false issue.

The issue is not whether any particular individual will find it worthwhile to run the gauntlet to get into public office. Each person can decide that for himself or herself. The real issue is the effect of all this on the quality of people who run the government—and therefore on the quality of service the government can provide to the public.

To serve the public, the government needs people with all the intelligence, honor, foresight, integrity, courage and wisdom it can get. People with these qualities have many other options available besides political or bureaucratic careers. In order to get a job, they do not need to grovel before congressional committees, pander to the press, or be sanctimoniously savaged over every triviality that can be rhetorically blown up in the media.

There is not such a surplus of people with all the relevant qualifications that we can afford to drive many of them away by making government careers unattractive, or the entry to them splattered with mud, tangled in red tape, and surrounded by a mine field.

Worse yet, we do not want the government run by people who pant for elective or appointive office so much that they will endure any disgrace and comply with any demand, just so that they can get their hands on the levers of power. It's bad news for all of us if those are the kinds of people who end up running the show in Washington.

The sheer complexity of many laws regulating elected and appointed officials makes it difficult for anyone to be sure he or she has obeyed them all. Even Senator Howard Metzenbaum, the most sanctimonious attacker of those nominated to appointive office, was embarrassed by revelations that he himself had violated some of the innumerable federal guidelines. But it barely caused him to pause for station identification before resuming his holier-than-thou routine.

In the movie *Casablanca,* the cynical police chief said: "Round up all the usual suspects." When a qualified nominee they happen to disagree with appears before a Senate confirmation committee, you can depend on some members of the committee to round up all the usual rhetoric.

The irony is that the numerous disclosure requirements, election campaign laws, and witch-hunting committee hearings have done nothing to make government more honest. As long as politicians have hundreds of billions of dollars of the taxpayers' money to hand out in exchange for votes and campaign contribution, the fundamental corruption will remain.

—June 23, 1986

Homosexual Politics

Hundreds of babies have died of AIDS. A nun has recently died of it from a blood transfusion. This deadly disease is not confined to homosexuals and drug addicts. They are exporting it to the general population.

At one time, societies had the common sense to try to

protect themselves from those with lethal, contagious, and incurable diseases. That was before deep thinkers substituted rhetoric for reality and before the homosexual lobby became politically powerful.

The big concern in the media is not that innocent people are dying from a disease due to the behavior of others. The big concern is that homosexuals, drug addicts, and others not be "discriminated" against because of "hysteria" over AIDS. Terribly clever editorials and cartoons have ridiculed those who would rather be safe than sorry.

Although AIDS is a newly discovered disease still being studied, there are a remarkable number of absolute statements about how it is not contagious in the usual ways—even while new ways in which it can spread are still being discovered. This absolute certainty often comes from hospital and school administrators dependent upon politicians, and from politicians with an eye on the homosexual political lobby. Independent medical researchers who have spent years studying AIDS are not nearly so certain. Some of these medical researchers recently testified in court against the New York City decision to let children with AIDS attend public schools.

Why are children with much milder contagious diseases kept out of school, but not children with AIDS? This disease has already killed half the people ever known to have it, and with no cure in sight for the other half, who are living on borrowed time. The schools' decision cannot be explained on medical grounds but is readily understandable on political grounds. Mothers of children with measles or scarlet fever are not organized politically, but homosexuals are.

Eye doctors have been medically advised to wear gloves when examining patients with AIDS because the tears are a possible source of contagion. Yet when nurses in San Francisco hospital wanted to wear gloves, they were forbidden to do so. Not advised—forbidden. You don't upset the homosexual lobby in San Francisco.

The mere screening of blood transfusions for AIDS has been blown up into a civil rights issue. Any reluctance to scatter AIDS patients among other hospital patients is considered a terrible violation of human rights. The right of the other patients not to have to worry about AIDS does not count.

Neither do the rights of parents who do not want to send their children to schools where they might catch AIDS. These parents' protests are ignored, and they are treated as if they were yokels or fascists. "The era of segregation is over!" New York's top school administrator announced grandiloquently. The Board of Education keeps it a secret which schools have AIDS students attending. In other contexts, that's called stonewalling.

Meanwhile, homosexuality is being taught in so-called "sex education" courses as just another "lifestyle." One of the great, tragic frauds of our time has been the name "sex education" for courses that indoctrinate fad thinking on sex, behind the backs of the parents. These courses are not about biology but about ideology, and the lifestyle they talk about is becoming a death style.

The homosexual political lobby depict themselves as a downtrodden minority. But they are not seeking to be left alone in peace. They already have that. Most people neither know nor care what they are doing.

Far from being downtrodden victims, homosexuals are well-heeled, well-placed, and vindictive against anyone who dares to criticize them in any way. Homosexual politics is not about protecting individuals' rights to be left alone. Homosexual politics centers upon the promotion of their way of life in public, in the media, and in the schools, to a captive audience of other people's children. It is about the symbolic glorification of homosexuals and homosexuality. It is not about their right to associate with each other, but about destroying other people's rights to decline the association, and to keep their children away from them in schools or in children's organizations.

The fact that we take their "civil rights" rhetoric seriously is a sign of how we have been conditioned to respond automatically to certain rhetoric, the way Pavlov's dog responded to the ringing of a bell.

—September 11, 1985

Another Crisis

"**D**o you know how many times Americans had their feet bitten by alligators last year?"

"No."

"3,618,524."

"Is that the number of feet or the number of people?"

"I think it's the number of feet bitten by alligators. You divide by two to get the number of people."

"What if the same alligator bit the same person's foot more than once?"

"Well, I guess that would reduce the number of people a little further, but I think you are missing the point."

"Wait a minute. It could have been just one alligator biting one person 3,618,524 times."

"You are being frivolous about a crisis."

"A crisis? Says who?"

"The A.C.T.—the Alligator Crisis Team."

"Who are they?"

"A group of concerned citizens who have formed a public interest organization to help victims of alligators."

"How do they help? Do they jump on the alligators and pull them off the people?"

"Don't be ridiculous. They engage in programs of public awareness, therapy for the victims, collection of information and statistics, and public interest lobbying to get good laws and policies in areas where there are alligators."

"Do they get paid for this, by any chance?"

"Well, they have to eat, like anybody else."

"In other words, they make a buck out of all this?"

"But they're not in it for the money. They're a non-profit organization."

"What difference does it make whether the money they get is called profit or something else?"

"You're being very difficult."

"No, I just want to know who these people are who make money by throwing a scare into us about alligators."

"You're looking at this all wrong. There's an alligator crisis and they are performing a public service by making us aware of it."

"How do I know there's an alligator crisis?"

"They tell you."

"I know a used car dealer who tells me he's got a great bargain for me, but I don't believe him."

"That's different."

"Who collects all these statistics that they throw around?"

"Why, they do. That's part of their public service."

"But the bigger their numbers are, the more money they can expect to get, right?"

"I don't know why you keep talking about money, when I've already told you they're a non-profit organization."

"But the more scared they can make us, the more we donate, right?"

"Well, I would certainly hope that more public awareness would lead to increased private donations and more government funding."

"Oh, they get their hands in the taxpayer's pocket too?"

"I can see it's hopeless talking to you. Where would we all be if everybody had your attitude?"

"We would have fewer people running around trying to scare the daylights out of us—and we would have more money in our own wallets."

—August 29, 1986

V

THE LAW

Legalized Blackmail

"**T**he power to tax involves the power to destroy." Chief Justice John Marshall was not against taxes when he said that. He was simply warning us how dangerous that power was if not kept within limits.

In our time, the power to litigate has become the power to destroy. Much-needed housing, factories to provide jobs, and power plants to generate electricity, have all been destroyed by litigation. It was not that the people who wanted to build these things were found guilty of violating some law. It was just that the litigation dragged on so long that the costs became too much to bear. If you can delay a $10 million project for three years by litigation, at a time when the interest rate is about 10 percent, then you have cost the builder more than $3 million.

It doesn't matter if a court finally decides that he isn't guilty of anything. He is still out $3 million. People who want housing and jobs also lose—and may be less able to afford their loss.

It is hardly surprising that this kind of situation lends itself to blackmail. Often it costs very little for one person to tangle someone up in legal proceedings. Some high school kids in their spare time were able to block a multi-million-dollar development in California by raising "environmental" issues.

The judge suggested that the issue be settled out of court. The developer gave the teenagers $50,000 worth of land and $100,000 in cash, so he could get on with his work.

Environmentalist organizations are well aware of the power of delay through litigation. A handbook from one environmental organization openly refers to lawsuits as "an effective delaying tactic" which can "force the developer to abandon his plans due to financing difficulties."

139

The key factor in this game is that it costs one side far less than it costs the other to keep legal proceedings going. Anybody can make up a list of terrible things that might happen to the environment if anything whatsoever is done. Some organizations specialize in this kind of calculated hysteria.

There are all sorts of environmental agencies at the state, local, and national levels that hold hearings on these complaints. When it comes time to put up or shut up, every charge may be exposed as hogwash. But that doesn't stop the very same charges from being made again before another agency or in court. And when they are shown to be hogwash again, that doesn't prevent an appeal.

Some judges seem to regard the remotest chance of an injustice as intolerable. Therefore they allow interminable legal proceedings, which can produce even greater injustices.

Local politicians get into the act too. If you want to build a housing development, a factory, or an office building, it may not be enough that you have faithfully complied with thousands of regulations. It may be suggested that you also build a bicycle path or a park for public use at your own expense. Why? Because if you don't, they may decide to hold hearings or have a study done on the "environmental impact" of your project.

It doesn't matter what these hearings or studies will find. What matters is that they will take time—and that you may be paying interest on millions of dollars in borrowed capital while they drag on. Often it is cheaper to build whatever they want built, and try to tack the cost onto the rent charged the tenants.

Sometimes what they want is so costly that it is cheaper to cancel the whole project and take your losses now, before they get bigger. If you are a big-time developer, such losses may be just a normal cost of doing business. If you are someone who wants a home or a job, it may not be that easy.

The people who play these environmental games usually have homes and jobs already—often very large homes and very well-paying jobs. They may not want their view spoiled, or their property values reduced, by grubby things that serve ordinary people. Or they may just like the idea of being out where the deer and the antelope play—but not children.

It is an aristocratic kind of selfishness that imagines itself to be far-seeing and concerned about the higher things. Environmentalists often speak of "preserving" places for posterity.

What they mean is that future people like themselves should have the same privileges over the common herd that they have.

The power to litigate often gives them the power to destroy anything that would disturb their particular vision of the world.

—May 3, 1985

Judicial Activism

Recently judges have launched some bitter public attacks on those who criticize judicial activism. U.S. Supreme Court Justice William J. Brennan has led the way in these public attacks, and California's controversial Chief Justice Rose Bird has followed his example. Editorial writers and law professors have rallied to their cause.

"Judicial activism" is a fancy phrase for a very plain thing. When the law says A and the judge wants it to mean Z, he "interprets" it as meaning Z. Deep thinkers may call that judicial activism. Back where I come from, we call it lying.

Judges don't just twist and stretch the law for fun. Usually they do it to promote some article of faith in the liberal creed. That's what wins them the support of the media and academia.

Attempts to justify judicial activism are very complicated and very clever. But they boil down to the kind of excuses any parent of a small child should be used to hearing.

With small children and judicial activists alike, the first excuse is that they didn't know you didn't want them to do what they did. Judicial activists and their supporters claim that the original intentions of those who wrote the Constitution are "unclear." But it so happens that the people who wrote the Constitution of the United States were very straightforward writers—much clearer than most law professors. As with some children, however, the problem is not that the judges don't know what the rules are, but that they don't want to follow them.

The ploy is to say that no one knows exactly what is meant by Constitutional phrases like "due process" or "cruel and unusual punishment." If you want to play that game, no one knows "exactly" how far it is from the Washington Monument to the Tower of London. When you get the distance in miles, you can say that's not exact, because you want it in inches. And when you get it in inches, you can say that's not exact because it's not accurate to a millimeter. There's no limit.

But if you use the fact that no one knows "exactly" how far apart they are to argue as if they are only about three blocks apart, or over a million miles apart, then you are lying—or engaging in judicial activism, as deep thinkers say.

This is the game that Supreme Court Justice William Brennan played when he said, "We cannot know *exactly* what the Framers thought 'cruel and unusual punishments' were"—as he reversed a death penalty decision as "unconstitutional." What the Framers of the Constitution clearly did *not* mean was the death penalty. They explicitly mentioned the death penalty in other parts of that document.

All the states that ratified the Constitution had death penalty laws. The first Congress that ratified the Constitution also passed federal death penalty laws—afterwards. Pious talk about how hard it is to know exactly what the writers of laws meant is almost invariably used to justify things that they clearly did not mean.

Judicial activists like Brennan play the same game with the phrase, "due process." This legal expression was already hundreds of years old when it was first written into the U.S. Constitution. For Supreme Court justices and law professors to pretend to wide-eyed innocence as to what it means at this late date is a little much. Of course, no one knows "exactly" what it means. But for centuries it never meant that criminals had to be turned loose if the cops didn't advise them that they could stonewall.

You don't need to know "exactly" how tall the Washington Monument is to know that it's taller than you are—and that any statement to the contrary is false.

When the innocent act fails, judicial activists fall back on the fact that change has occurred since the law was passed. "Change" is a magic word used to justify decisions that have nothing whatsoever to do with change. The most famous—or notorious—Supreme Court decisions of the past generation have had no relationship to any of the many changes that have occurred since the Constitution was written.

Death penalties are still death penalties, abortion is still abortion, segregation is still segregation, libel is still libel, and arresting a criminal is still arresting a criminal. And lying is still lying.

—February 21, 1986

Prayer in Schools

We all need many moments of silent meditation after the recent Supreme Court decision on school prayer. Instead, we are getting a great deal of political noise from all sides.

The court ruled that the government cannot institute prayer—even silent prayer—in a public school, though it can establish a moment of meditation, which the individual can use for any purpose he chooses. This may be a reasonable policy, in a religiously diverse society with wide ranges of beliefs. But, whether such a policy is reasonable or not, the larger question is whether the courts should be making policy or applying the Constitution. Sometimes there is a twilight zone between the two. But that does not mean that all 24 hours consist of twilight.

The increasingly bitter struggle over school prayer is a symptom of a wider and more dangerous social pattern—the utter loss of mutual forebearance, on which the viability of civilized society depends. This loss of forebearance has by no means been limited to religious fundamentalists. Secular fundamentalists have in fact led the way in stretching the First Amendment far beyond anything meant by those who wrote it. The famous "wall of separation" between church and state appears nowhere in the Constitution. It is one of those endlessly repeated clichés that substitutes for evidence, logic, or common sense.

When the Constitution forbad an "establishment or religion," it was not talking about some abstract or arcane principle. It was talking about something very concrete and familiar to those who wrote the Constitution. Britain had an established church. That meant that the government supported it with the taxpayers' money and that members of that church had certain legal privileges de-

144

nied to members of other churches or to people not religiously affiliated. The First Amendment to the Constitution
forbad the Congress of the United States from doing the
same.

The Constitution did not say anything about the federal
government's having to be "neutral" between religion and
agnosticism. It did not even prevent individual states from
having their own established churches, if they wished.
Only the federal government was forbidden from imposing a national church or interfering with individuals' beliefs. As Chief Justice Warren Burger pointed out,
the very Supreme Court that issued this decision began its
day with an invocation of prayer, just as both Houses of
Congress do.

As a policy issue, you can say that imposing prayer on
children in school is different from having a chaplain invited to pray before an assembly of adults—and powerful
adults at that. But as a question of what the Constitution
does and does not prohibit, that is irrelevant. If the "wall
of separation" or government "neutrality" between belief
and unbelief is not imposed on Capitol Hill, it is inconsis-
tent—if not dishonest—to claim that the same Constitution
imposes these secular dogmas in the school house.

Insofar as the Constitution distinguished between the
federal and state governments in such matters, it left the
states free to do things that Congress was explicitly forbidden to do. Within the past generation, however, judges
have extended various Constitutional prohibitions from
the federal government to the state governments. In many
areas, they have added extensions to the extensions, until
they improvised a whole shanty-town of judge-made doctrines around the original Constitutional structure. The
thrust of such developments in the school prayer cases has
been to drive religion out of the public schools.

The merits of such a policy could and should be debated
as a policy. But the pretense that the Constitution required

it has only dishonored the Supreme Court and embittered the give-and-take of democratic policymaking.

Religious fundamentalists have likewise shown little forebearance toward those who do not share their views. With ample opportunities for daily prayers—at home, at church, or individually even in the public schools—why force other people's children to be part of a public ceremony that may or may not represent what they believe? The word "voluntary" is simply dishonest when you are talking about a public school teacher leading little children in prayer.

The drive to impose one vision on everyone is the antithesis of the forebearance that the American Constitution represents. But it is the one thing that both sides of this struggle have in common. Far better if our laws provided vouchers, tax credits, or other devices that would put religious schools within the financial reach of those who believe in them. These children could begin each day with genuine prayers while secular schools could begin the day without them—and neither would be subjected to such politically inspired evasions as moments of silence.

—June 11, 1985

The Right to Smear

Now that Ariel Sharon has lost his libel suit against *Time* magazine, the press can relax. The truth will not have to cramp their style.

The right to smear remains intact.

The jury decided that what *Time* printed was false and

that it defamed General Sharon. But the magazine escaped on the third requirement for libel—that the statements be made "maliciously" or in "reckless disregard" of the truth.

The story insinuated that General Sharon aided or abetted the massacre of innocent civilians. Moreover, it claimed that this was the conclusion reached in the appendix of the Israeli government's secret Kahan report.

It would have been despicable and unforgivable if Sharon had in fact done what they claimed. The jury decided that he had not. The Israeli government supplied the secret Kahan report to the court. It did not contain what *Time* magazine claimed it said.

Some people would say that this case had a good ending. Sharon's reputation was vindicated but *Time* magazine did not have to pay out millions of dollars. Therefore there was no "chilling effect" on the rest of the press.

From Sharon's viewpoint, that may be all right. Perhaps two out of three isn't bad.

The larger question is how the enormous power of the media can be abused with impunity. You or I could live a lifetime of decency and honor, and see it all smeared away with one paragraph in a publication that reaches millions of people around the globe. And most people on the receiving end of the smears cannot do anything about it—not even carry on a lawsuit like Sharon's.

How many people can travel 10,000 miles, spend months in court, and get a government to release a secret document? And with all that, he lost.

While declaring that there was legally no libel, the jury took the unusual step of saying that the *Time* reporter "acted negligently and carelessly" in handling the story. But somehow that did not mean that the magazine itself had "reckless disregard" of the truth or falseness of what it printed.

Let Union Carbide try to say that it is not responsible for

what its employee did halfway around the world, and see how many journalists buy it.

Time magazine has already issued an incredibly self-righteous statement that the case should never have been allowed in the courtroom, and that they have "the utmost confidence in our editorial staff and our editorial procedures." Although the Israeli document they cited did not contain what they claimed it contained, *Time* assures us that other secret documents must have it. Unless Israel is to become the only nation on earth without any confidential documents, *Time* can make any claim it wants to, without fear of being proven wrong—again.

The issue of press responsibility goes beyond particular individuals who are smeared. The public's "right to know," which editorial writers talk about so piously, should include the right to know that what is presented to them as fact is in reality third-hand gossip and speculation. ·

If *Time* magazine had lost this lawsuit, it would not have stopped anybody from printing rumors and speculation. They would just have to call them by their right names, instead of letting them masquerade as facts.

This might close down some of the scandal sheets you find near supermarket check-out lines. But reputable publications would just have to clean up their act. Is truth-in-labelling a "chilling effect"?

The *Time* magazine case is even worse than the case between CBS and General Westmoreland, which is still going on. The claim in Westmoreland's case is that CBS ignored evidence that went against their preconceived ideas, and broadcast only what supported their political bias.

But plain old bias is not falsehood. If Westmoreland wins and Sharon loses, will that mean that you can publish outright falsehoods but cannot edit interviews to suit your own taste? If both lose, does it mean that anything goes?

Make no mistake about it—sensational stories mean big

money. Unless it also costs big money when they are false, we can expect to continue to see free-wheeling smears and insinuations masquerading as news.

The righteous indignation of the media against chemical polluters will always ring hollow, as long as they claim a constitutional right to pollution of the facts. That is what a virtual exemption from libel action amounts to.

—January 25, 1985

The Sears Case

Sears Roebuck was one of the first big companies to have "affirmative action" plans, nearly 20 years ago, to try to add to the number of its minority and female employees. As a result, they were also one of the first to be sued by the government for discrimination, using the very statistics that Sears had collected to help monitor its own efforts to recruit women and minorities.

This was by no means the first time that those who tried to do the right thing were singled out as targets, just because it was easier to make a case against them. The government's case against Sears was based on statistical "under-representation" of women among Sears' commission salesmen, who sell such items as furnaces, roofing, fences, automobile tires, and men's clothing.

Time was when common sense would have told you that many women were unlikely to gamble their livelihoods on making commissions selling such items. But common sense doesn't carry much weight, now that we have statistics.

Many judges accept statistics so gullibly that it is possible for the government to prosecute a discrimination case without a single human being who claims that he or she was personally discriminated against. That is virtually what the Equal Employment Opportunity Commission did in the Sears case. But this time they ran into a judge who couldn't be snowed with numbers.

Judge John A. Nordberg pointed out in his recent decision that, with eight years of voluminous evidence on a company with over 900 stores, the EEOC was "unable to produce even one witness who could credibly testify that Sears discriminated against her."

The judge ruled in favor of Sears. His decision included a lengthy and penetrating discussion of statistical analysis and its pitfalls, which should be required reading for other judges, Congressmen, and media deep thinkers.

If it was a farce for the EEOC to have brought this case in the first place, the outraged responses to the decision were a bigger farce. Women's liberation "spokespersons" denounced it as a setback for equal rights. The American Civil Liberties Union protested. All the usual liberal editorial writers said all the usual liberal things.

At the heart of the controversy is the grand dogma of our times—that people would be evenly distributed everywhere, if it were not for institutional barriers. No speck of evidence has ever been advanced for this sweeping assumption. Dogmas don't need evidence.

The cold fact is that almost nobody is evenly distributed anywhere or ever has been—whether in the United States or abroad, in this century or in past centuries. Anyone who watches basketball must know that there is an uneven distribution there that makes other uneven distributions look like nothing. Yet blacks have no power to discriminate against whites in basketball. Back in the days of the Roman Empire, 10,000 Britons were killed in a battle with the Roman legion—who lost less than 500 men. That's what the lawyers call "disparate impact," but it is not clear who could be charged with discrimination.

Nowhere do people have the same preferences, behavior, or performance. Italian immigrants and their descendants have not been evenly distributed, even in Italian neighborhoods. Whether in Buenos Aires, Boston, or New York, people who originated in the same parts of Italy have tended to cluster together on the same streets overseas. Among people of Japanese ancestry in Brazil, most of those originating in Okinawa marry other Okinawans—not people from Tokyo, much less members of the Brazilian population at random.

Neither military forces nor college students are random. Most of the sergeants in the Soviet army are Ukrainians. When Nigeria became independent, the bulk of the enlisted men in its army came from northern tribes, while the bulk of its officers came from southern tribes. Hispanic American college students do not choose the same mixture of subjects to major in as Asian Americans, and the Asians in turn do not choose the same subjects as whites, or whites the same subjects as blacks.

You could fill volumes with similar examples from all over the world and throughout history. Some differences are striking to the eye because the people are of different color or sex. But even where they are physically indistinguishable, the differences are enormous.

Where did we get the idea that people are homogeneous, and therefore could be expected to be evenly distributed? From intellectuals. Anybody else would have too much common sense.

—February 14, 1986

Chances versus Guarantees

It costs a lot less to buy a raffle ticket, giving you a chance to win a new car, than to pay for guaranteed delivery of the same car. You don't need a Ph.D. from the London School of Economics to understand why.

But too many judges seem to miss the difference between a chance and a guarantee. People who bought homes in a quiet little town often become resentful when other people begin moving in, expanding and changing the community. They pass laws depriving other people of the right to buy and sell property freely. The excuse for depriving other people of their rights is that the people who were there first came to enjoy an atmosphere and lifestyle that will no longer be the same if they can't keep others out.

What the original people paid for when they moved in was a chance for a particular way of life—not a guarantee. If they wanted a guarantee, they would have had to buy up the surrounding property as well. Instead, they go into court to get a guarantee free of charge.

American laws call for equal treatment and property rights. Yet people who happen to have been in town first are treated as more equal than others. Judges wave aside both the equal-treatment principle and property rights, in order to transform the chances that were originally bought into permanent guarantees. From an economic point of view, it is the same as if judges declared that everyone who bought a raffle ticket is entitled to a car.

Something similar often happens when people buy or build a home near an airport. They may get a home cheaper in that location because of the noise. Then they go into court and complain about the noise.

Maybe the airport has expanded or the planes have gotten louder. Those are among the chance factors involved when you buy a house next to an airport.

If the people were there first and an airport was suddenly built in their midst, then it makes sense to force the airport authorities to compensate them for the mass destruction of the values of their homes. Such values are just as real as the value of the land that has to be paid for to build the runways.

It is not just a question of justice to individuals. From the viewpoint of society as a whole, the most efficient use of resources is promoted by forcing those who use them to pay their real values to others—not values mis-stated by legal or political fiat. When judges give guarantees to people who paid only for chances, they are grossly mis-stating the costs to others and to society as a whole. Raffle tickets cost a lot less than guaranteed delivery.

So-called "consumer advocates" likewise try to turn chances into guarantees. If I buy a used car or a low-budget version of any product, I pay less—precisely because the chances of problems are different from what they would be with a brand-new, top-of-the-line, state-of-the-art product. Product liability laws that turn chances into guarantees give a brief windfall gain to those consumers holding these products when the laws and judges' ruling go into effect. Afterwards, all consumers have to pay higher prices to cover the costs of increased product liability. They are forced to pay for guarantees, whether they want them or not.

Some of the product liability laws and courts cases hold the manufacturer responsible, even if the customer completely misused the product contrary to instructions. At first this hits the manufacturer. But ultimately it hits the other customers, in the form of higher prices, so that people who are careful with the product end up subsidizing those who don't use common sense. It also reduces the incentives to use common sense.

Many judges seem so enamored of their roles as Robin Hood on the bench that they do not look beyond the immediate effect of their turning laws into means of judicial largesse. But there are no free lunches. As long as chances cost less than guarantees, somebody is going to have to pay the difference. Usually that is the public.

—June 14, 1985

Supreme Court Cop-Out

Every time the U.S. Supreme Court comes out with a new decision on so-called "affirmative action" policies, deep thinkers begin to gather around to read the tea leaves, to see what it could possibly mean. It is a little like trying to figure out Rubik's Cube.

In the *Bakke* case, back in 1978, the Supreme Court ruled that it was unconstitutional for the University of California to reject a white applicant to one of its medical schools while setting aside places for minority students with lower qualifications. Apparently reverse discrimination was wrong. But only apparently.

A year later, in the *Weber* case, the same Supreme Court ruled that it was all right to deny a white worker admission to a company training program while accepting blacks with lower qualifications. After several more cases going back and forth on the issue, the Supreme Court, on May 19th of this year, ruled that it is illegal for a school board in Michigan to lay off white employees with more seniority while

retaining minority employees with less seniority, even
though it is done to preserve racial balance and maintain
"role models" for minority youngsters.

Well, which is it, fellas (and Mrs. O'Connor)—legal or
illegal? We don't want to be nosy, but it would be nice to
know what "the law of the land" is.

Lawyers and judges may say that these were all very
complex cases which cannot be "oversimplified" as mere
judgments on affirmative action. These Supreme Court
decisions were complex, all right. Nothing is more complex than avoiding the obvious. Anyone who has followed
the reasoning of the Flat Earth Society knows that it is
much more complex than the reasoning of those who say
that the earth is round.

The real issue is not complexity but contradiction. If you
read the Constitution as requiring equal treatment of individuals, then you may as well forget about equal group
statistics. Those who play by the same rules repeatedly end
up with drastically different results, whether they are playing baseball, investing in the stock market, or taking a
course in physics. Huge group differences are the rule
rather than the exception, in countries around the world,
and regardless of whether there is much discrimination,
little discrimination, or no discrimination.

By the same token, if the Supreme Court wants to go the
group statistics route, then it may as well forget about
treating each individual equally. The real problem is that
the Court wants to have it both ways—a sort of dry wet-
ness, cold heat, or stationary speed. One symptom of the
confused vacillation that goes with attempts to do mutually
contradictory things is that affirmative action cases not only
tend to produce 5–4 decisions but also fragmented opinions among both the majority and the minority.

By now, the arguments for and against preferential
treatment have been made at all intellectual levels, at all
emotional levels, and at all decibel levels. If the law is not

to be a mockery of uncertainty, the time is long overdue for the Supreme Court to bite the bullet and say yes or no, so that everyone can know what is and is not illegal. Instead, they are saying, in effect: "Keep sending us these cases one by one, and we will see if we can't scrape together five votes, one way or the other."

Every day some businessman has to make a decision that can determine the fate of his business and the future of his family. Every week some athletic coach has to make crucial choices, in a matter of moments, often on nationwide television, and in an occupation where it is a very short step from glory to unemployment. Is it too much to expect tenured Supreme Court Justices to have the guts to make up their minds?

Of course it will be hard, fellas (and Mrs. O.). But the taxpayers aren't paying your salaries, and giving you that big marble building to ramble around in, for nothing.

—June 2, 1986

Police Shootings

Understanding the limitations of human beings is the beginning of wisdom. But the New York Court of Appeals has demonstrated once more that many appellate judges recognize no such limitations in themselves, and are prepared to second-guess the limitations of everybody else.

In a case where all concerned were caught in a tragedy not of their own making, a huge mentally deranged woman wielding a knife attacked policemen who had been sent to get her. She was larger than most football players, and all efforts to reason with her, or to keep her at bay, failed.

During the struggle, she was swinging a 10-inch knife at an off-balance policeman when another officer fired twice with his shotgun. The woman fell—and later died.

The policeman's split-second decision to fire has now been second-guessed for more than two years—in the safety and comfort of court chambers and newspaper offices. The fact that the policeman was white and the woman was black was tailor-made for the media hype that followed.

"Detached reflection cannot be demanded in the presence of an uplifted knife." That remains as true today as it was when U.S. Supreme Court Justice Oliver Wendell Holmes said it 65 years ago, in a case where race was not an issue.

That is how the trial court saw it as well, when the policeman was first charged with manslaughter. The trial judge dismissed the charges. But the New York Court of Appeals has now over-ruled the trial judge (and another appellate court), so the policeman must go to trial on manslaughter charges.

The key issue from a factual point of view is whether the second shot was necessary. Second-guessers often seem amazed that an "unnecessary" number of shots are fired in such situations—situations they have never faced. The *New York Times* has repeatedly harped on "the second shot," just as the *Los Angeles Times* repeatedly expressed its shock that eight shots were fired by two policemen in a similar case a few years ago.

Such comments betray an ignorance of the realities of shooting—and an arrogant disregard of that ignorance when indulging in condemnation. As a former pistol instructor in the Marine Corps, I can assure these second-guessers that the kind of shooting precision or certainty they expect is seldom found, even in the peace and calm of a pistol range, much less in the heat of instant life-and-death decisions.

In the real world, it is not uncommon for criminals and the police to fire many shots at each other without any of them hitting the target. When a shot does hit, no lights go on to let you know it, the way they do in a video arcade. Only after the body is autopsied does anyone know how many bullets hit.

Policemen do not fire and then call "time out" to size up the situation before deciding whether to fire again. When a second's delay can mean the difference between life and death, you keep firing until it is clearly safe to stop. Two shots are hardly a shooting spree, in this context. Even after being hit a second time, the huge deranged woman was still able to fight against medical personnel who tried to help her.

Much has been made of the fact that the first shot so injured her hand that she should not have been able to hold a knife, in the opinion of medical examiners. Even assuming that they are right—that a slow-motion replay would show the woman no longer a danger after the first shot—the fact remains that the officer did not have the same amount of time that the medical experts had to determine her condition.

How much time did the officer have between shots? Estimates varied among the witnesses. A neighbor said the shots were "like bam, bam, one right behind one another." The longest estimate was "three to five seconds" between shots.

Some journalistic Sherlock Holmes at the *New York Times* has seized upon this longest estimate to imply that the policeman had time to realize that the second shot was "unnecessary." But obviously no one was holding a stopwatch—and people's estimates of very short time intervals are notoriously unreliable. Yet, on this flimsy basis, a much-decorated policeman who volunteered for hazardous duty is to be charged with manslaughter.

Is it not enough that such men put their lives on the line

in impossible situations? Must their lives and their honor be further jeopardized by editorial office heroes who blithely demand the superhuman, miles from the scene of the action?

No one should kid himself that undermining the police somehow helps the minority community. No other community has suffered more from the undermining of law enforcement over the past two decades.

This is only one of many areas in which the whole society is paying a terrible price for the moral preening of a relative handful of glib and self-infatuated writers.

—December 2, 1986

A "Rehnquist Court"?

Now that Antonin Scalia has been confirmed as the newest Justice of the Supreme Court and William Rehnquist has been elevated to Chief Justice, some will begin calling this "the Rehnquist Court." It is not.

There was such a thing as "the Warren Court," for the late Chief Justice Earl Warren had a talent for taking most of the Supreme Court in the direction he wanted them to go—even when that meant going far beyond what any Court before them had done, and often far beyond what the Constitution authorized.

There was no "Burger Court" in the same sense, for Chief Justice Warren Burger often found himself in the minority on the major Supreme Court decisions of his era. Although the so-called "Burger Court" was considered more conservative than the Warren Court, it did not undo the work of its predecessors. On the contrary, it continued drifting to the left—but at a slower pace and with a few halts.

It was, after all, during the Burger era that the death penalty was severely restricted and laws against abortion declared unconstitutional. We are still living with the legacy of the Warren Court—not just its specific decisions but also the general disposition of courts at all levels to go beyond the written law to ad lib social policy on their own moral grounds.

Both Rehnquist and Scalia have opposed such judicial activism. But Rehnquist was on the losing side of the Supreme Court's votes more often than not, and Scalia only replaces Burger, who was often on the losing side with Rehnquist. In terms of the "liberal" versus "conservative" line-up of votes on the Court, nothing has changed.

When you go beyond those pat labels, however, some small change has occurred, and larger changes may be down the road. As Chief Justice, Rehnquist is expected to be a more effective manager and strategist than Burger was, but the concrete effects of that may be small unless and until he gets a couple of more like-minded Justices appointed by this president or a future president.

Scalia's replacing Warren Burger may not leave things completely unchanged, even though both are usually labelled "conservative." Scalia has more of the intellectual strength and toughness required to resist the prevailing winds of legal fashion, which blow from the leading law schools to the highest courts in the land.

The constant chant from law professors and their followers among intellectuals and in the media is for judges to go further in shaping the law according to notions of morality and "social justice," instead of being tied down by the written words of the legislation or of the Constitution. Justices who follow this seductive chorus are likely to be lionized by academic intellectuals, and applauded in editorials across the country. Justices who resist and stick to the laws as written are certain to be depicted as people who "don't care" about "human values" or are too stupid to understand the higher morality. They are certain to be ridiculed in the law reviews and may even be called "racists" or "sexists" in some cases.

Being a "conservative" is not enough to enable an individual to resist all this. It takes a penetrating mind to see through all the pretty words and enticing arguments. And it takes strength of character to buck the winds of fashion. As a judge on the Court of Appeals, Scalia has already demonstrated that he has both.

Justice Harry Blackmun came on the Supreme Court many years ago bearing the "conservative" label. However, he has often voted with the liberal wing of the Court, led by Justices Brennan and Marshall. It was Blackmun who wrote the decision claiming that state laws against abortion were unconstitutional. More recently, he tried to claim that state laws against sodomy were unconstitutional.

The Supreme Court's role is not to decree whether abortion laws or sodomy laws are good or bad, but whether the Constitution permits the states to pass such laws. However, to the Brennans and Blackmuns, to say that they don't like a particular law is virtually the same as saying that they should declare it unconstitutional.

The legal havoc wreaked by more than 30 years of this kind of sloppy thinking and self-indulgent moral posturing will take a long time to repair. It will not be enough to put more "conservatives" on the Supreme Court, if they are mediocrities like Harry Blackmun.

Fortunately, there are some outstanding legal minds available. Court of Appeals judges Robert Bork and Richard Posner have shown both great intellect and great strength, and not just in their judicial roles. They came to the bench after years of tough battles in the academic world, where they not only bucked the tide but forced major changes in people's thinking in both law and economics.

There are far better people waiting in the wings than there are sitting on the Supreme Court. That is the most hopeful sign for the future. But the old holdovers, now in their 70s and 80s, are holding on for dear life, lest Ronald Reagan appoint different kinds of people to replace them.

After decades of producing legal chaos—reflected across the social spectrum, from staggering crime rates to the liability insurance crisis—these superannuated justices have somehow managed to convince themselves that they are indispensable. Few seem to want to follow Chief Justice Warren Burger into retirement.

They need to heed the words of Cromwell: "You have sat too long here for any good that you have done. . . . In the name of God, go!"

—September 22, 1986

VI

EDUCATION

Tough Teachers

Noted black economist Walter Williams traces his educational advancement to a time when he was chewed out unmercifully by a white teacher in a Philadelphia ghetto high school. Stung and angered at the time, Williams now says that the chewing out was richly deserved. More important, it turned him around. His grades shot up, he went on to college, eventually received a Ph.D., and now holds an endowed chair as professor of economics.

How many white teachers today are going to chew out a ghetto high school student—and perhaps do him one of the biggest favors of his life? For that matter, how many teachers of any race are going to chew out any student anywhere?

First of all, there are the dangers of retaliation from the student, his parents, the principal, or the courts. Besides, the prevailing dogma in education is that students must "feel good about themselves" and that "stress" must be avoided at all costs. After a couple of decades of treating children as if they were fragile as tissue paper, the net result is that Johnny can't read and can't think—but often has a presumptuousness that deep thinkers call maturity.

It wasn't always like this. My English teacher in junior high school was from the General Patton school of education. You could be any color of the rainbow and she would still give you hell if you didn't shape up.

She didn't care whether your home was broken or bent. Not once did she ask compassionately whether I had a nickel to ride the trolley to school or had to walk the whole 15 blocks. What she let me know was that I had better be there on time—and with my homework done.

A California psychiatrist who went to that same school

165

in New York tells me that his secretaries over the years have commented on the fact that he seldom misspells a word. My secretaries have made the same comment. If they knew Miss Simon, there would be no great mystery as to why.

These teachers were not cruel. What would have been cruel would have been to jolly us along and send us out into the world unprepared. The teacher who chewed out Walter Williams was a dedicated man who came to school early, so that he could tutor some ghetto youngsters who were trying to prepare themselves for college. Although I never saw Miss Simon's softer side (and never suspected she had one), my psychiatrist friend tells me that she and another teacher used their own money to take him to see a Broadway play, so that he could get a glimpse of a wider world than he saw on the streets of Harlem.

Like many ghetto youngsters, I never finished high school. A lot of rough years followed. But when I finally got myself together to try to go to college, I was able to score higher on the English portion of the entrance exam than the average Harvard student. Miss Simon had done her job. Who knows where I would be if she hadn't?

Dedicated people have not vanished from the human race. But we have made it hard for them to function or to survive in the public schools. A teacher who wants to come in early and tutor students can get into trouble with the teachers' union or the school administration. Marva Collins was hassled for doing that when she taught in the public schools. That was one of the reasons she set up her own school. A teacher like Miss Simon would today be the target of every "students' rights" activist and of lawyers from the American Civil Liberties Union.

A student's greatest right is the right to an education. Whatever interferes with that right has to go—whether it is his own immaturity, the disruption of other students, the incompetence of teachers, or half-baked social experiments. Otherwise, even the sweetest and most sanctimonious talk only conceals an unnecessary cruelty that will undermine him for years afterward.

—January 13, 1986

Mathematically Eliminated

The Rand Corp. and the Rockefeller Foundation have produced a report that should be required reading for precisely those people most likely to ignore it—crusaders, the media and politicians. Sue Berryman of Rand has compiled and analyzed a mass of statistical data on why women, blacks, Hispanics and American Indians are "under-represented" in science and mathematics—and why Asians are "over-represented."

Ms. Berryman traces the story back long before members of these groups show up in the job market. For some, any chance that they might have of a career in science or math is over before they finish high school. The pool of youngsters who are interested in science and mathematics, and who do well in them, is constantly declining, *from seventh grade on.*

It is sobering—if not grim—to think of teenagers as "has beens" with no realistic chance of a comeback. But that is what the evidence says, as far as math and science careers are concerned. Mathematics is the basic foundation for the sciences, and the battle for mathematical skills is fought and won—or lost—early on. The losers almost never become scientists, engineers, economists—or mathematicians.

Some lose by default. Girls do about as well as boys in math up to the ninth grade. At that point, many courses become "elective"—and girls don't elect math as often as boys. By the time they both take the college entrance examinations, the boys have pulled ahead in math, though the girls more than hold their own in English.

From that point on, they are on different tracks, heading in different directions. People may speak mystically of the need for "role models" or wax indignant about employer discrimination. But the cold fact is that serious study of mathematics, science, engineering or economics is off-limits to most young women by the time they set foot on a college campus. It is a closed case long before they reach the employer. No amount of "role models" can substitute for the prerequisites for Calculus I.

Nor is time changing this pattern. The difference between male and female test scores on the quantitative portion of the Scholastic Aptitude Test was larger in 1982 than in 1972.

Differences among racial or ethnic groups in their preparation for scientific or mathematical careers are even greater than male-female differences. High school seniors who are black, Hispanic or American Indian average lower math scores than do seniors who are white or Asian. However, these gaps (though larger than the male-female gap) have tended to decrease somewhat over time. Blacks, for example, have the lowest math SAT scores, but their math scores have also risen the most between 1977 and 1982. The math scores of whites actually declined slightly during the same years.

The Rand study shows black, Hispanic and American Indian college students under-represented in fields requiring mathematics—notably the physical sciences and engineering—and over-represented in fields that do not, such as education. These patterns persist—and accentuate—in post-graduate study. Ph.D. holders of different racial and ethnic backgrounds receive their doctorates in a vastly different assortment of fields.

Only about 10 percent of the Ph.D.s received by blacks are in mathematically based fields, such as science and engineering. For Asians, well over half their doctorates are in such fields. Asians receive 17 percent of all Ph.D.s in engineering, though only 4 percent of all Ph.D.s in general. Among engineering doctorates, Asians outnumber blacks, Hispanics and American Indians—put together—by more than 5 to 1. This is truly staggering when one realizes that blacks alone outnumber Asians many times over in the general population.

One of the encouraging signs to emerge from Ms. Berryman's study is that college students whose parents also went to college do not differ nearly as much by race or ethnicity when it comes to specializing in mathematically based fields. Differences among black, white, Hispanic and American Indian college students in this respect are very small in the second generation, though Asians are greatly over-represented relative to all of them. Unfortunately, the Rand study presents no data on the second generation's preparation or performance in these fields.

There are many implications that might be drawn from this study. For example, the reigning dogma that group differences in "representation" are due to employer bias could hardly survive scrutiny in the light of these data. But that is not the thrust of Ms. Berryman's argument at all. Instead, she devotes herself to earnest proposals for increasing female and minority representation in the sciences, for "correcting representational imbalances," in her words.

Why it is *incorrect* for people to make their own choices in the light of their own aspirations, performances and competing goals is a larger question never addressed. This is, after all, a Rand Corp. study done for the Rockefeller Foundation, and one wonders what role there would be for either organization if people started thinking like that.

It must also be noted that this report has all the other earmarks of think-tank and foundation reports—a blah cover, a wholly uninformative title ("Who Will Do Science?") and a subtitle that says what it is actually about—if you can stay awake long enough to read all the way through the long subtitle. The report itself is a gold mine of information drawn from a wide variety of sources.

—February 8, 1984

College Athletes

You may have heard the one about the college athlete who won five letters—but had to have someone else read them to him. Unfortunately, that is too close to painful reality to be funny.

Of this year's 18 first-round draft choices of the National Basketball Association, less than half graduated from the colleges they finished. Not one majored in math, English, philosophy, engineering or any of the sciences and most majored in recognized "gut" subjects. This is a long-standing pattern among college athletes in other sports as well.

While a relative handful of these youngsters will get dazzling salaries when they turn pro, most college athletes will not be chosen in any round by any professional team. More than 90 percent of college athletes never sign a pro contract.

Add to this the fact that most college athletes do not get a degree—not even in Mickey Mouse subjects—and it is clear that the vast majority, whom you never hear about, have pathetically little to show for four years of their life down the tube. They have simply spent four years providing entertainment for their classmates, affluent alumni, media audiences, and for paying customers in the stadium.

The rationale is that college athletics is an "amateur" activity. Where else can you bring in a million dollars on a single Saturday afternoon and still call it an "amateur" activity? It is tax-exempt, too. This is a better racket than the mafia. Why would anyone become a mafioso if he could be an athletic director instead?

The coach's salary may be in six figures and the college may make millions, but if a few dollars manage to trickle down to the athlete who puts his body on the line, that is regarded as a scandal. The real scandal is not in those penny-ante payments under the table but in what goes on openly all the time.

Nowhere else are organizations legally permitted to collude in a cartel, in order to pay nothing to those who work for them. Yet colleges who recruit the disadvantaged offspring of poorly educated families as athletes are allowed this exemption from the law. The anti-trust laws would annihilate any cartel that even attempted to do half of what the National Collegiate Athletic Association (NCAA) does all the time.

Doctors, lawyers, and other well-educated people can take care of themselves. But still the government would stomp on any group of hospitals or law firms that colluded to lower the pay of doctors or lawyers. Only with the most vulnerable and inexperienced young people does the law look the other way by not subjecting the NCAA to the same rules.

The colleges' pious explanation of unpaid athletes who bring in big bucks at the box office is that they are receiving an "opportunity" for "education." This explanation wears pretty thin when you realize that most of these athletes don't get a degree—and that those who do often squeak by in meaningless courses. The kinds of academic standards applied to athletics was revealed when Creighton University managed to keep one of its basketball players going for two years, even though he couldn't read. He finally had to go back to *elementary school* to learn to read! A faculty member who protested against lower standards for athletes at the University of Georgia was fired.

Any sports fan knows that a disproportionate number of both college and professional athletes are black. Athletics provides a way for some to escape poverty and enter a world they would never see otherwise. Tragically, however, it creates the illusion of far more opportunity than actually exists. There is a grand total of less than 3,000 blacks in all professional sports put together, including coaches and trainers. This is nothing for millions of black youths to rely on.

Belatedly, the NCAA has made some small efforts to clean up its act. It has ruled that athletes entering college must have a total of 700 points from their verbal and math scores on the Scholastic Aptitude Test, in order to be eligible to play.

What does that amount to? Well, technically it is 700 points out of a possible 1600. But SAT scores do not start at zero. You get 400 points just for showing up, so it's really 300 points earned out of a possible 1200 points earned. We're not talking about Rhodes Scholars.

Unfortunately, some civil rights leaders have denounced the new NCAA rule, saying that it's "racist" to force black students to meet such standards. I think it is racist to say that they can't meet the standards. Colleges who want good teams will have no choice but to bring these youngsters up to the requirement, perhaps by tutoring them in the summer before they enter. It may be the only decent education they will ever get.

—July 7, 1986

Teachers' Salaries

One of the pious things that gets said over and over again in newspaper and television editorials is that we should pay our public schoolteachers higher salaries. Sometimes the claim is that they are doing an important job. Sometimes the claim is that they are paid less than some other occupation that requires less education.

Both claims sound good the first time around, but neither will stand up under scrutiny. We ought to start paying attention to the facts before we start paying out more of the taxpayers' money.

There is no denying that teaching the next generation is an important responsibility. But that also means that a rotten job of teaching is even more disastrous than a rotten job in some other areas. Moreover, those who do a rotten job of running a store or a restaurant are likely to find themselves going bankrupt, while those who do a rotten job of teaching are likely to find themselves with tenure for life, and maybe moving up to become rotten principals, if they have enough seniority. At the very least, they can expect regular pay raises, the longer they keep messing up our children's education.

A California teacher officially certified as incompetent was recently offered an extra $40,000 to take early retirement (complete with pension, of course), because the cost of trying to fire her could have been even greater. When incompetent teachers are too young to try this approach, it is not uncommon for them to be transferred somewhere else. When the parents at the new school finally realize how terrible the teacher is and set up a howl, a new transfer is arranged. This musical chairs scenario is so common that it has a name: "The dance of the lemons."

The schools that are most likely to get rid of bad teach-

173

ers are those where the parents are affluent, well-educated, articulate, and influential. The schools that are most likely to get stuck with real losers teaching their kids are schools in neighborhoods where the people are less fortunate, where the parents can be ignored—and where a decent education is the child's only hope for a better life.

But while the very worst teachers are likely to end up where they can do the most damage, the whole public school system has been deteriorating across the board. Falling test scores for two decades have been accompanied by rising grades—and rising propaganda about how this was "the brightest and the best" generation of students. It was only after the public became outraged that some few changes were made to stop the decline. But we are still not back where we were.

The first response of the education establishment to the criticism of falling test scores was denial and lying. Teachers' unions and educational administrators dismissed the tests as "irrelevant." Then they claimed that the Scholastic Aptitude Test scores were going down because so many new disadvantaged students were now going to college that they lowered the average. This was a lie.

It was not just the average that was going down. The absolute numbers of students scoring in the top brackets were also falling. The average SAT scores at many of the top colleges and universities are still lower than they were 20 years ago.

Even those who acknowledge that the schools have failed seem to think that paying more money to teachers will attract better people into the public schools. Ordinarily this would make sense, if we were talking about an occupation where people are recruited from an open and competitive labor market. But the teachers unions, educational codes, and teachers colleges have done their best to prevent this from being an open and competitive market for talent.

The cold fact is that anyone wanting to become a permanent, tenured teacher in most public schools has to have taken so-called "education" courses. These Mickey Mouse courses have been a bad joke on campuses across the country for many years. Serious, intelligent students avoid them like the plague. The late James B. Conant's classic survey of schools of education called them the "intellectual slums" of the university. Students majoring in education have long had the worst test scores of students majoring in any field. Yet this is the pool from which we are supposed to draw better teachers by paying higher salaries.

Many private schools get better teachers while paying lower salaries than the public schools. Private schools are not required to limit their selection to people who come from the intellectual slums of education courses. They can hire people with degrees in mathematics to teach mathematics, people with degrees in chemistry to teach chemistry, and people with other degrees in real subjects to teach those subjects.

You can throw all the money you want at a poorly qualified pool of people and still not get a good teaching profession out of it. Before trying to wring more money out of the taxpayers, perhaps it is time to start looking at the barriers that keep good people out of teaching—and the rules that keep rotten teachers in the classroom long after they have demonstrated their incompetence.

—October 18, 1985

Chicken Little in Academe

Make no mistake about it. The special interests are going to fight tooth and nail to keep the taxpayers' money flowing into their pockets. And if they succeed, the huge federal deficit can only be reduced by raising taxes again.

No one is fighting harder for their federal subsidies than academics. Their advertising isn't even called advertising but op-ed columns, written by college presidents, professors, and other well-cared-for members of the educational establishment. As a public service, they tell us why our money should go to them.

Students are the pawns in this game. Economically, students are merely the conduits through which other people's money reaches administrators and professors. A large part of that money comes from government, even in so-called "private" colleges and universities.

An experienced full professor at Stanford averages more than $50,000 a year in the School of Education and more than $100,000 in the School of Medicine. This does not of course include their research grants, secretaries, travel expenses, sabbaticals, and other goodies.

The picture we are presented in the media is that students have to have more government aid because tuition and other college expenses are rising by leaps and bounds. It is as if rising college tuition is one of those things that just happens, like rain or earthquakes.

But one of the big reasons why tuition has skyrocketed out of sight in the past quarter of a century is precisely because government—state and federal—has been willing to pour more and more billions into academia to help cover rising tuition costs. Having the government subsidize anything is virtually a guarantee that the price will go up.

Colleges can't raise tuition unless somebody is going to pay it. In many cases, that somebody is the taxpayer—and not just for state schools.

The state of California alone has increased its subsidies to Stanford students by more than ten-fold, over the past quarter of a century. Federal Pell grants that didn't even exist a quarter of a century ago have poured more than a million dollars in a single year into Stanford, not counting federal loans and numerous other subsidies.

And Stanford is a private university, as they will tell you with great unction. Public universities get even more from the taxpayers.

Back in 1959–60, only 27 percent of Stanford students received financial aid. That doubled to 54 percent by 1984–85. The total aid received has increased twenty-fold.

With this kind of money available, why wouldn't the tuition rise? Why wouldn't professors get 50 or 100 grand for nine months work?

Academic public relations discourage even thinking about it in such crass economic terms. After all, a university is a "non-profit" organization, serving noble purposes.

Maybe. But many a small businessman would consider it a good year if he received the kind of money a single tenured professor has guaranteed to him every year for the rest of his career. The businessman would probably be willing to take the money, even if it carried the tainted name of "profit," without the sanctimonious aura of academia.

Like so many who speak ringingly of "the poor," academic spokesmen have their own big bucks at stake. The issue they raise is whether "the poor" will be able to continue to go to college if federal aid is reduced.

But only "the poor" whose family income is over $32,000 a year will be cut off. The poor are once again used as a red herring.

It's not a question of how many students can go to college but how much they can be charged. No college can afford to make drastic cutbacks in the number of its students, either directly or by charging tuition that few can pay.

Too much attention has been focused on the issue of whether the students live too high on the hog. It is not basically a question of how well the students live, but how well the professors and college presidents live, and how many campus boondoggles can be continued.

Stanford is of course only one of thousands of colleges and universities across the country receiving government aid in numerous forms. The taxpayers are subsidizing the competition of all these institutions for faculty members— driving up not only salaries but grants, time off with pay, and many other goodies. The question is whether the public will continue to pay for all the rising bids—and the rising tuition that goes with them.

—September 10, 1985

Staff Infection

Of all the fatuous things said by college commencement speakers each year, none is more poisonous than the idea that there is something higher and nobler about a career in so-called "public service."

People in many occupations serve the public: grocers, doctors, bus-drivers, telephone repairmen. Indirectly, so do farmers, factory workers, and in fact everyone who produces a good or a service that others use. But when the

deep thinkers speak of going into "public service," with
that special unction in their voice, they mean becoming a
bureaucrat or politician.

The vision that is unfurled to the departing graduates is
one of self-sacrifice for the common good. This is con-
trasted with going into the grubby world of business to
make money for yourself.

Why it is nobler to seek power over others rather than
be a producing part of the economy is never really explained. But it doesn't have to be. After four years of
listening to "social scientists" tell them how bad this country is, many students may feel that rescue is urgently
needed.

Some of the graduates may want to go out and apply the
theories they learned from their professors. (God help us
all.) But, more than specific theories, students have been
presented with a vision in which "thinking people" have to
assume responsibility for the rest of us poor slobs.

Not as many students are buying this as in the 1960s.
But the professors are still selling it and the media are still
echoing it.

It is a very self-flattering vision, in which the Olympians
up on the hill look out for the peasants down in the valley.
Some even consider it democratic and patriotic.

The young men and women who follow this vision into
the bowels of the bureaucracy, who join the staffs of politicians or become clerks to judges, seldom realize how
profoundly ignorant they are of the society they want to
help rule.

True, they may have learned some things in school that
the man in the street does not know. But the mechanic,
the builder, or the policeman also understands many
things that the student and his professors are blissfully
ignorant of.

A great civilization requires a staggering range of knowledge, skills, and insights that no individual can possibly

master, outside a narrow circle of his own specialty. Intellectuals are the last people to realize their own vast sea of ignorance surrounding the small island of their knowledge. That is why they are so dangerous.

No small part of the political mess that graduates are urged to help clean up was caused by previous generations of graduates going boldly out to save a world they knew pathetically little about. Their insulated lives on college campuses were often followed by insulated lives on the government payroll or in non-profit organizations.

Neither of these kinds of organizations has to meet the test of performance. Both deal in words that need only sound plausible to the right people.

The staffs of Congressmen, judges, and both government and non-profit bureaucrats are filled with these bright young people, inexperienced in the real world that exists beyond their narrow, inbred circle.

The growing load of responsibilities put on legislators, judges, and heads of government agencies make them ever more dependent on staffs whose own knowledge is secondhand, theoretical, or ideological. When a judge has to decide an anti-trust case against a corporation, how likely is his staff to contain someone who has actually run a corporation and knows what it is like from the inside? The judge is far more likely to have to turn to a young law clerk, whose head was pumped full of theories of corporations in college or law school.

The dependence of Congressmen on their staffs is notorious. With all the politicking and public relations that Congressmen have to do, there is no way that they can find time to really look into all the things they have to vote on. Staffs do that—and people who have vast amounts of real world experience are unlikely to be on those staffs.

It is the blind advising the blind. And sometimes it is the biased advising those with the same bias.

Urging college graduates to go into so-called "public

service" is urging them to continue the insularity and presumptuousness that college breeds. For society, it means aggravating a condition that might well be called staff infection.

It is especially inexcusable for the idolizing of "public service" to be promoted by a college or university. Higher education is supposed to teach people to see beyond surface glitter and plausible words. It is supposed to see beyond the fads of today to the broad sweep of history. Much of history is the story of how political leaders have squandered the blood and treasure of the human race.

—May 31, 1985

Illiteracy Hysteria

Three accountants were being interviewed for one job. The employer gave each of them the same set of figures and asked them how large his profit was.

The first accountant gave his answer. The employer shook his head. That accountant didn't get the job.

The second accountant came up with a different interpretation of the figures. He didn't get the job either.

The third accountant said: "How large do you *want* the profit to be?" He got the job.

Numbers games are also being played with illiteracy rates. Illiteracy in the United States is less than 1 percent according to some figures and more than 30 percent according to others. There are still other figures in between, and you can have the numbers be almost as large or as small as you want, depending on how you define literacy.

There is more literacy if you define it as the ability to read a street sign than if you define it as the ability to read Shakespeare. All sorts of off-the-wall tests of "literacy" are used to generate inflated numbers. Some have long, rambling sentences containing words like "recertification." Author Jonathan Kozol calls you illiterate even though you can read, if you "read only at a level which is less than equal to the full survival needs of our society." How is that for precision? Kozol picks up an extra 35 million people with this definition.

A canny old lawyer once advised a young attorney: "When your argument is weak, shout louder." Kozol does a lot of loud shouting, with overblown rhetoric about "survival" and the like.

Deep thinkers in the media have seized on inflated "illiteracy" statistics to generate more hype. Television is especially effective at dramatizing false generalizations. All they have to do is find one person who is genuinely illiterate and conduct an "in-depth" interview, detailing all the problems he has because he cannot read. The viewer is then left with the impression that this is typical of the huge numbers of people labelled "illiterate" because of off-the-wall tests and vague definitions.

When confusion and panic are being spread on a large scale, there is usually some reason—and that reason often involves big bucks. The current hysteria-mongers are talking about needing many billions of dollars to set up programs to deal with the "crisis." Sound familiar?

The centerpiece of the "illiteracy" hysteria is a book called *Illiterate America* by Jonathan Kozol. On the cover, it claims that one out of every three Americans cannot read this book. And the other two shouldn't, according to Ben Wattenberg, who has exposed many statistical fallacies and frauds over the years. Anyone familiar with Kozol's previous writings could have predicted what the bottom line would be—that this is a terrible society, which can be redeemed only by turning money and power over to the Jonathan Kozols of the world.

Many in the media were suckered into becoming the mouthpieces of special interests with programs to finance, empires to build, and ideological visions to promote. But media people have been easy marks precisely because their own vision is so similar to that of Kozol and his compatriots. In that vision, American society is mean-spirited to the poor, insensitive to children, and stubbornly resistant to peace with the Soviet Union.

Anything that fits into that pattern gets a sympathetic hearing in the media, and often gullible acceptance. Anything that contradicts the media's underlying assumptions will be lucky to be heard at all, even if it has twice as much statistical data, with ten times the accuracy and validity of Kozol's figures.

A massive statistical analysis was published last year, showing that female and minority students were grossly under-prepared for study in mathematical, scientific, and technical fields. It was totally ignored by the media and sank into oblivion without a trace. But anyone who wants to claim that minority and female under-representation in these same fields is due to employment discrimination can get center stage on the 6 o'clock news any day of the week.

The mindset behind the current "illiteracy" hysteria was revealed by the head of an outfit calling itself "Push Literacy Action Now." He spoke of "people who feel very cheated by the system that miseducated them." If there are people who grew up in a country with free, compulsory education who blame "the system" after they didn't bother to learn, then it shows how far we have gone in denying personal responsibility, laying guilt trips on "society," and thinking that wringing more money out of the taxpayers is the answer to everything. This mindset is far more wide-spread than illiteracy, and does far more harm.

Does American education need improvement? Absolutely. Will the "illiteracy" hysteria help? Not bloody likely. Many of our present educational problems are due to the same kinds of politicized hokum.

—October 28, 1986

Academic Freedom at Hillsdale College

One of the real battles for academic freedom is being fought by a little college in central Michigan. Its opponent? The federal government.

Hillsdale College has about a thousand students and a proud history of independence that goes back to 1844. This isn't the first time they have tangled with the federal government.

Back during World War I, the U.S. Army wanted Hillsdale to segregate the one black student in their R.O.T.C. unit. Hillsdale refused, took the case to Washington, and won.

This was in keeping with the college's tradition. Hillsdale's original charter in 1844 declared that it be open to all persons, "irrespective of nationality, color, or sex."

Ironically, the federal government has now been pressuring Hillsdale for the past 10 years to file "affirmative action" reports and submit to the many regulations and paperwork this involves. Hillsdale has refused. The case has been in the courts.

Nobody has charged Hillsdale with racial or sexual discrimination. The feds just don't like the idea that some little college in Michigan can tell them to mind their own business.

It so happens that the first Michigan woman to receive a Bachelor of Arts degree received it at Hillsdale in 1852. The first woman to become a college trustee in Michigan was also at Hillsdale.

Blacks were graduating from Hillsdale back in the middle of the nineteenth century. Some of these early graduates had been born slaves. When the "affirmative action" enforcers demanded to see photographs of the first black student to graduate from Hillsdale, they were told that blacks graduated from Hillsdale before photography came along.

Long before "affirmative action" began, Hillsdale College decided to steer clear of federal control by refusing to take any government money. This was back in the early 1950s, when most academics (and other deep thinkers) pooh-poohed the idea that federal aid to education would mean federal intrusion into the running of colleges and universities.

When the feds started demanding to see Hillsdale's numbers and percentages by race and sex, they were told that the college received no federal money, and therefore did not have to comply with the regulations that went with the money. You would think that would be the end of it— if you didn't know bureaucrats.

Someone found an ingenious technicality. Some of the Hillsdale students received veterans' benefits or borrowed money under government loan programs. That made the college "indirectly" a recipient of federal money.

If you buy this line of reasoning, then the local supermarket is a recipient of federal funds, whenever someone buys groceries with a Social Security check. By this reasoning, federal employees are violating the separation of church and state whenever they put money in the collection plate on Sunday.

Hillsdale did not buy it. They couldn't see why they had to file forms just like someone who received grants from federal agencies.

Unfortunately, the Supreme Court bought it. Another college that refused federal money—Grove City College in Pennsylvania—was told that its students' receipt of federal aid made the college subject to the same rules as if it had been taking federal grants.

Hillsdale is now trying to raise scholarship money privately, so that its students won't even have to take federal aid to which they are entitled.

If Hillsdale isn't discriminating, then why is it putting up this big fight?

It may be hard to explain to people who have never been on the receiving end of the red tape and petty requirements that go with "affirmative action." It's not just whom you admit to college or hire to work for you, but how many procedures and delays, and how much paperwork you go through in the process.

Some years ago, the personnel department where I worked was very upset with me because they didn't think I jumped through all the right hoops, in the right order, when I hired someone for my research project—even though the person hired was a black woman who was easily the best qualified applicant.

But it is more than not wanting to be hassled. It is not wanting Big Brother looking over your shoulder and getting deeper and deeper into your decisions with every passing year.

With all the Reagan Administration's talk about getting the government off people's backs, you might think they would stop the feds from hounding Hillsdale College. It would have been the perfect opportunity to come to the defense of an institution with clean hands.

Instead, they tried to get the Internal Revenue Service off the backs of Bob Jones University, which in fact has racist rules for students. The principle was the same but the administration could not have picked a worse example.

It is a sad example of what happens to common sense in Washington.

—February 14, 1985

Academic Storm Troopers

Academics are forever discovering problems with society and offering their solutions. Meanwhile, they are ignoring a problem of cancerous proportions in their own profession.

The scene: Northwestern University. Adolfo Calero, an opponent of the Marxist Sandinista dictatorship in Nicaragua, is preparing to address an audience that has come to hear him speak. But before he can deliver his speech, a group of people storm onto the stage, throw red liquid on him, and seize the microphone from him.

One of these disruptors is a member of the faculty. She shouts into the microphone: "He has no right to speak here tonight, and we're not going to let him speak. He'll be lucky to get out of here alive."

Shocking incidents of this sort have erupted from Harvard to Berkeley. What is even more shocking is that faculties and administrations have come to accept it. Northwestern was the exception, because the provost refused to grant tenure to the young woman who took part in these storm trooper tactics. The college faculty has been up in arms—against the provost.

The head of the local chapter of the American Association of University Professors has denounced the provost's action as persecution of a faculty member for her left-wing politics. A faculty panel looking into the matter did not condone the disruption, but recommended that, instead of being let go (in 1987), the professor should have received a "severe reprimand and warning"—along with tenure, which would have made it all meaningless and a mockery.

The unwillingness of academics to take any serious action against radical storm trooper tactics was epitomized by an official of Wellesley College, who said that the "level of disruption was reasonable" when a speaker was shouted down and had eggs and blood thrown at him on that campus. There have even been nationwide campus organizations formed which openly assert their right to disrupt campus speakers and prevent them from speaking, by whatever means are necessary. Yet the outcry among academics is not against these organizations, but against the organization Accuracy in Academia—which *reports* such incidents to the public.

When Secretary of Education William J. Bennett recently sounded an alarm about the cancerous intolerance on many college campuses, the academic smoothies tried to bury his statement under pious and misleading comments.

The dean of the college at the University of Chicago said: "I do not recognize the description of American universities presented by Secretary Bennett as any university I'm familiar with." He must not have heard of Northwestern University, right outside Chicago.

The head of the Association of American Colleges said that Secretary Bennett's statement "sounds exaggerated to me," and the president of the American Association of University Professors said that only "a tiny minority" of students and faculty fit Bennett's description.

But that is the whole point—that a tiny minority of zealots has been permitted to undermine or destroy the free flow of ideas to the majority. Nazi storm troopers were "a tiny minority" in Germany, as the Communists have been in all the countries they have taken over.

Colleges are more calm today than in the 1960s. But on too many campuses, it is the calm of capitulation. People whose views are likely to set off the radical storm troopers are simply not invited.

A lack of guts alone cannot completely explain the inaction of campus officials and faculty. They can be very active—and very severe—against even peaceful protests by conservative students. A Yale student who put up posters parodying the posters that campus homosexuals had put up was suspended for two years—and threatened with permanent expulsion if he did anything similar when he returned. The dean of Yale's own law school called the suspension "outrageous." Several Dartmouth students have been dealt with in similar fashion for their counter-demonstrations against pro-divestment students.

A conservative student newspaper at the University of Texas had to go into court for a restraining order to get the university administration off its back. The courts also had to be resorted to—and also successfully—by student newspapers at the University of Oregon and the University of San Diego.

The quiet acceptance of double standards and ideological intolerance on many campuses demonstrates how hopeless it is to expect academia to clean up its own act. Taxpayers, parents, donors, and others will have to demand to know what is going on before there will be a free flow of ideas.

—September 5, 1986

The Fight over School Vouchers

Now that a new effort is being made in Congress to provide school vouchers for low-income children, the education establishment is responding with the old smokescreens and evasions.

First of all, they claim that the public schools are improving, and deserve "another chance" before we experiment with vouchers. Unfortunately, that "improvement" consists of regaining only a fraction of the vast decline in test scores that has taken place over the past quarter of a century.

The national goal for 1990, set by the U.S. Department of Education, is to raise the Scholastic Aptitude Test scores up to where they were back in 1972. No one is optimistic enough to hope that the scores will rise to where they were in 1963, at least not any time soon. Maybe in the twenty-first century.

For a long time, the education establishment denied that any decline in standards was taking place. Grades were rising while scores were falling and there was much pious talk about this being "the brightest and the best" generation of students ever.

Test scores aren't everything, they say. In fact they said it a lot when the facts became widely known. But if you judged by how well the students could think, the situation was even more disastrous. Teaching at UCLA—where students are above average—during the 1970s, I often wondered what they could possibly have been doing for 12 years of schooling before reaching college. Even many bright students had no conception of systematic logical thinking.

190

In a debate on education (scheduled to be broadcast the first two weekends of May on "Firing Line"), the head of California's public education system, Bill Honig, repeatedly called for "another chance" for the public school system before trying vouchers. But vouchers and the public school system are not mutually exclusive. The public schools have never been denied a chance to do better, nor will they be. What a voucher system would do is give them an incentive as well as a chance.

Attempts to depict vouchers as a dangerous experiment ignore the fact that freedom of choice already exists in vast areas of American life. It is the public school monopoly which is an exception. It is "another chance" to continue as an unopposed monopoly that the education establishment is really asking for.

Much is made of the fact that the public schools in the past Americanized generations of immigrants. So did the Catholic schools, which Irish, Polish, and other immigrants attended. Are Irish Amerians or Polish Americans any less American today?

Under all the honeyed words and hokey propaganda, this is yet another of those age-old battles over power. If there is any universal lesson in history, it is that those with power always resist letting others have freedom. In the public school monopoly, money as well as power are at stake.

A self-serving bureaucracy with iron-clad tenure can be expected to fight tooth and nail against having to compete with private schools that offer a better product at about half the cost per student. Do not be surprised if some low blows are thrown in such a contest.

One low blow is the claim that it will cost some enormous amount to have vouchers. In reality, when students go from a high-cost system, like the public schools, to a lower cost system, like the private schools, the costs to the country go down, not up. Most private schools are not Andover or Exeter, just as most public schools are not Beverly Hills High School.

Another low blow is the claim that the public school system will be "destroyed," and we will be risking everything on an untried private system. For this to happen, there would need to be an immediate and vast exodus from public schools, a boarding up of schools all across the country, and a quick sale of buildings and grounds. This scenario insults everyone's intelligence.

Parents are not about to yank their children out of well-functioning public schools just because there are vouchers, nor could private schools accommodate them all immediately if they tried to. As with everything else, some parents would choose different schools—both public and private—and some would leave their children where they are. Some private schools would expand and some new ones would be created. But it all takes time and there is nothing irreversible about any of the decisions made.

The building of apartments has not caused single-family houses to disappear. Both are still being built everyday. Nor has the manufacturing of sports clothes caused suits to become extinct. More books than ever are being produced today, despite the availability of television, movies, and other media.

When the education establishment runs around like Chicken Little yelling that the sky will fall if vouchers become available, they betray either an ignorance of free competition or a contempt for the intelligence of other people.

—April 17, 1986

VII

RACE

Lessons from Sri Lanka

News reports on the civil war in the island nation of Sri Lanka seldom mention how that bloody conflict got started. Its roots go back to preferential treatment policies—what we in the United States call "affirmative action."

The two main groups on this large island off the coast of India are the Sinhalese majority and the Tamils, who are the largest minority. Although both groups originated in India, they have been on the island for centuries.

The Tamil minority, concentrated in northern and eastern provinces, happened to be located where European and American missionaries began establishing schools, back in the colonial era, when the island was called Ceylon. Many Tamils received more and better education than the Sinhalese. Not surprisingly, they became "over-represented" among civil servants, doctors, lawyers, judges, and engineers. In addition to these native Tamils, there were large numbers of other people from India who created much of the industry and commerce of the island, and were therefore "over-represented" among business owners.

This ethnic imbalance caused no great trouble during the colonial era, when the British held power in the country. But when the colony of Ceylon became the independent nation of Sri Lanka, right after World War II, things began to change.

The Christian, English-language schools that had produced much of the Westernized leadership class in the country were bitterly resented by the Buddhist, Sinhalese-speaking majority. Once independent, they began to use their political muscle to oppose Western culture, religion, language—and the Tamil minority.

195

Preferential treatment in favor of the Sinhalese people and culture began in the schools, the universities, and government. When double standards for admission to the universities were not enough to eliminate the "over-representation" of the Tamils, quotas were substituted. Tamils were 49 percent of all medical students in 1969 but this was cut back to 17 percent in just six years. Over the same span of time, Tamils were cut back from 48 percent of all engineering students to 14 percent.

Tamils were also driven out of the army, the civil service, and the teaching profession. Tamil businesses were harassed. The Tamil language was no longer acceptable in official business, even in areas where it was the language of the overwhelming majority of people. Government policy was supplemented by mob violence against the Tamils.

Moderate Tamil leaders tried to reason with the government. But Sinhalese politicians who had whipped up emotions against the Tamils were in no position to change course. The net result was that moderate Tamil leadership was quickly replaced by more extreme leadership, which demanded secession. Assassinations and sabotage began to back up Tamil demands.

Violence begat violence. Sinhalese army units ambushed in Tamil areas responded with indiscriminate vengeance against Tamil civilians. Tamil guerilla bases have been set up in India, and tensions between the two nations have risen.

The present government of Sri Lanka shows some signs of wanting to defuse tensions within the country and with India. But too much innocent blood has already been spilled on both sides for that to be easy. The toll of killings, devastations, and masses of homeless refugees has generated a bitterness going far beyond the original preferential policies that started it all.

If anyone had known in advance that such policies would lead to this disaster, would they have considered it worth it to try to produce an artificial ethnic balance? With the country still struggling to extricate itself from civil war, it is difficult to see where either group has gained anything on net balance.

—August 19, 1985

Preferential Treatment

If you think "affirmative action" is about preferential treatment for blacks, think again.

Blacks are only about 12 percent of the U.S. population. But more than 60 percent of all Americans are legally entitled to preferential treatment. Women alone are 52 percent of the population.

Moreover, the United States is not the only country with group preferences. Half the population of India is entitled to preferential treatment. So is more than half the population of Malaysia and Sri Lanka.

These preferential programs are all different. But they have certain results in common.

The first thing they have in common is that the preferences spread over the years.

Preferences in India began for the benefit of the untouchables, one of the worst-treated people on the face of the earth. But, over the years, preferences began to spread to all sorts of other groups. Together, these other beneficiary groups now greatly outnumber the untouchables.

Something similar happened in the United States. Blacks were used as the entering wedge. Then preferences spread to women, Asians, Hispanics, American Indians—and the end is not yet in sight.

Another similarity among preferential policies is that they usually end up helping primarily those people who were more fortunate to begin with.

In one state in India, the least fortunate groups—who were 12 percent of those entitled to preferences—received only about 1 or 2 percent of the jobs and college admissions given out by the preferential programs. The top groups entitled to preferences (11 percent) received nearly half.

In Malaysia, a study found that "at most 5 percent" of the Malays received benefits from preferential programs for all Malays. These tend to be the more prosperous, educated, and politically connected Malays. In Sri Lanka, preferential admissions to universities for people from backward districts went largely to affluent people living in these districts.

The story is not very different in the United States. Blacks with higher education and job experience have begun overtaking whites of the same description. Blacks without education and experience have fallen further behind than before.

People who believe in preferences and quotas claim that "equal opportunity" is just not enough. That is a very clever way of putting it. It does away with any need to compare the hard facts about the results of equal opportunity versus preferential treatment.

In the United States, minorities advanced more under equal opportunity policies than under preferential policies. A similar story can be found in Southeast Asia.

The Malays receive preferential treatment in Malaysia but not in Singapore. In both countries the Malays earn much less than the Chinese. But in Singapore the Malays are gaining ground, under equal opportunity policies, while in Malaysia the relative positions of the two groups are pretty much the same as before.

Preferences don't work—especially not for the masses.

But the fortunate few for whom they do work have made preferential policies a political sacred cow.

One of the most ominous parallels among the various preferential programs is that they all provoke "backlash" resentment. This backlash takes different forms in different countries.

In Sri Lanka, where the losers from these policies are geographically concentrated, there have been armed uprisings and demands for secession. In India, the backlash has taken the form of increasing violence against the untouchables. Hundreds are killed annually, amid rising denunciations of the preferences they are supposed to be receiving.

Malaysia keeps down open racial violence through extraordinary precautions. It is a federal crime even to criticize the nation's racial policies. The Malaysian government obviously knows that they are sitting on a powder keg.

We in the United States don't seem to realize that we too may be sitting on a powder keg. Preferential policies have not existed here as long as they have in other countries. We are still at the stage where there are only rumblings and a few disturbing signs—like racial hate groups gaining a foothold among the educated classes, or an openly avowed ku klux klansman winning a Democratic primary in California.

If—God forbid—this country ever goes the way of other countries torn apart by racial strife, those few people who gained from preferential policies will be the first ones on the jet planes out of here. The people in the ghettoes and barrios, who received little or nothing from these policies, will be the ones left behind to face the consequences.

—January 16, 1985

Some Lessons from Australia

Italians are one of the largest immigrant groups in Australia. A recent study showed that Italian-born women in Australia have only one child out-of-wedlock for every 148 births.

The same study says that these women have seldom received "sex education" and know little about contraceptives.

This contradicts everything our deep thinkers keep saying about the need for more sex education in the schools and massive international programs of contraception and abortion. Values do more to prevent teenage pregnancy and family disintegration than trendy talk and costly programs.

Those who make a living by stampeding us into hysteria are not about to look at hard evidence. That makes it all the more urgent for the rest of us to look at the facts before we get hypnotized by rhetoric.

Throughout the Western world, population growth fell sharply during the 1930s—long before "the pill" or sex education. When times were tough, people had fewer children. Back in those days, it was understood that you were supposed to support any children you brought into the world. People acted accordingly.

Sex education has been sold as a way to prevent teenage pregnancy and venereal disease. Both have skyrocketed after sex education has been introduced.

It is hardly surprising. Much of what is called "sex education" is nothing more than propagandizing school children with the latest fads in beliefs about sex. A captive audience of inexperienced young minds is turned over to

200

zealots for "the sexual revolution," to people who depict homosexuality as simply "an alternative lifestyle," and to all those who are more concerned with being "with it" than with being right. Parents and their values are treated as obstacles to "progress."

One ninth grade textbook says that sex between children and adults "usually" causes "no permanent emotional harm." How the author knows that—or can prove it—is beyond me. But who needs evidence? This textbook is used in Palo Alto, home of the deep thinkers from Stanford University.

The personal tragedies and social catastrophies that have followed from reckless experiments have all been blamed on other things. Runaway teenage pregnancy in the black ghettoes is blamed on "the legacy of slavery." Yet black teenage pregnancy was nowhere near this high before welfare payments turned it into an "alternative lifestyle."

Puerto Ricans have an even higher rate of teenage pregnancies than blacks, and they do not come out of a legacy of slavery. But the mass migration of Puerto Ricans to the U.S. mainland began after the welfare state was already in place. That is the common factor.

Mexican Americans are similar to Puerto Ricans in many ways, but Mexicans are not automatically citizens and their history of aversion to government puts additional barriers between them and the welfare state. Despite many cultural and economic similarities between Mexican Americans and Puerto Ricans, the Mexican Americans have far lower rates of teenage pregnancy or broken families.

Against this background, it is hardly surprising that Italians in Australia have extremely low rates of illegitimate births. In this "modern" and "progressive" age, few people have so maintained family values as the Italians, whether in Australia or elsewhere.

Italians are relatively recent immigrants to Australia— mostly since World War II—and so have below average incomes and education. Many are concentrated in poor neighborhoods. All these things are supposed to cause teenage pregnancy.

The fact that they don't causes no second thoughts among deep thinkers in Australia. They are in fact striving mightily to get the Italian immigrants drawn into the orbit of the welfare state. Fortunately, the Italians are resisting—and advancing on their own. Despite lower than average incomes, Italians in Australia own their own homes more frequently than the average Australian.

—October 18, 1984

Black "Leadership"

It is only beginning to be recognized by the media that the opinions expressed by black "leaders" are often the opposite of those of the black population. Recent polls showing most blacks opposed to preferential treatment and a rising proportion favorable to President Reagan have at least momentarily shaken the deep thinkers.

It is a long way from such opinion poll results to the election of black officials who no longer toe the line of the traditional civil rights organizations or echo the liberal-left rhetoric of the congressional "black caucus." Politics is not just a referendum on issues. Politics is a profession requiring organization, name recognition, and the kind of savvy that comes only with experience.

Most black politicians with such qualifications are products of an earlier era—the era of the civil rights struggle, which still has deep and powerful emotional resonances.

More and more independent black scholars are coming to see the civil rights approach as having already done its work, and now needing to be superseded by new approaches to other serious problems of the black community—of which massive teenage pregnancy and violent crime are among the most devastating. Yet, however intellectually correct these scholars may be, politics runs on other fuel.

No one can explain the emotional outpourings from the black community for Jesse Jackson's hopeless candidacy for the Democratic presidential nomination in 1980 without understanding what it meant symbolically to many blacks. No well-researched position paper on specific issues could ever have evoked a similar response. But now Jesse Jackson's candidacy is behind us. He may run again in 1988, but the newness of the experience is gone, and it will undoubtedly be harder for him to keep himself in the headlines.

What the Jackson candidacy and the emotional outlet it provided may have done is clear the decks for others who can now put issues in the center of the stage. Even so, it will not be easy for black candidates with a very different agenda to reach and gain the political support of the black community. Issues are not just issues. Some issues are symbols of group solidarity, and to break with traditional black leaders and traditional rhetoric on these issues can raise questions of loyalty and dedication, even among voters indifferent to the issues as such.

But before even reaching the voters, a candidate must first establish rapport with all sorts of community leaders—ministers and civic leaders, as well as politicians. Many of these are people for whom the civil rights era was one of the central episodes of their lives. The approaches that worked in that era will not be let go easily, even if those approaches have now passed the point of diminishing returns and become counterproductive.

On the other side of the scale, however, is the silent but

inescapable fact that new generations are constantly rising and old generations constantly passing from the scene. A majority of today's black population had not yet been born when the historic Supreme Court desegregation decision was announced in *Brown* v. *Board of Education.* Nearly half had not been born when the Civil Rights Act of 1964 was passed. As this group reaches adulthood and rises to leadership, it should become more feasible to put today's problems at the top of today's political agenda.

As it becomes more and more painfully clear that the taxpayers are not going to keep pouring money into new programs with sparkling promises, other approaches will have to be considered. The illusion that painful social problems can be blamed on Ronald Reagan's being in the White House will necessarily dissipate when the Reagan Administration is over.

The tragedy is that millions will suffer while this process is slowly unfolding and the rhetoric and programs of the past fight a rearguard battle against confronting today's reality. Polls indicate that the black population seems to be moving much faster toward this understanding than its "spokesmen" are.

—February 10, 1986

Malaise in Malaysia
Kuala Lumpur

Kuala Lumpur is the capital of Malaysia. But you would never know it by looking at the names of its stores, factories, and other businesses.

Chinese names abound on business signs, though the

Chinese are a minority in Malaysia. Foreign companies are also common. Hitachi and other Japanese firms have branches here. So do American companies. Malay businesses are the exception rather than the rule.

This is not an unusual situation in the history of nations and peoples. But it is no less painful to the Malays or politically dangerous to the Chinese. At one time, people from India owned most of the businesses in several east African countries. Western Europeans and Americans dominated many industries in czarist Russia. Jews, Armenians, and Lebanese have had similar economic prominence in various nations around the world.

In all these cases, however, local resentments have been fierce, and occasionally bloody. Malaysia is no exception. Malaysia's last great race riot occurred 15 years ago, when Malays unleashed an orgy of destruction and slaughter on the Chinese community. Things have been quiet in recent years—but at a price.

That price has been government-mandated discrimination against people who are not of the Malay race, regardless of whether they are citizens of the country. This racial discrimination is expressed politically as preferences or quotas for the *Bumiputras* or "sons of the soil." A citizen of Chinese or Indian ancestry is never considered a native son, no matter how many generations his family has lived in this country.

That means that anyone not of the Malay race faces official discrimination across the board—not just in government employment but also in private employment, university admissions, and in virtually every aspect of Malaysian life. In a multi-page advertisement in *Fortune* magazine, the Malaysian government openly declared to foreign companies that they would have to follow race-based employment policies in Malaysia.

Another part of the price of racial peace is a federal law against criticism of the nation's racial policy. It is literally a crime to protest. No such organization as the N.A.A.C.P. could exist legally in Malaysia. Foreigners have been expelled merely for trying to do research on Malaysia's racial policies.

Malaysia is a classic example of how the plain fact of economic differences among groups can be politically escalated into an issue that threatens the peace and stability of a nation. Generations ago, in colonial Malaya, poor and ill-educated Chinese immigrants came into the country to do much of the hard and dirty work in the tin mines and elsewhere. People from India were brought in to work on the rubber plantations.

By and large, Malays did not have to stoop to these kinds of jobs. They were peasants with their own land, in a country where climate and soil guaranteed them subsistence, without undue toil and with considerable leisure. They developed an easy-going, graceful, but economically inefficient way of life.

The Chinese came from a country where life was never that easy. In much of China, it was a full-time job to produce enough to keep body and soul together. The workaholic attitudes this produced have marked the Chinese in countries from Peru to Australia. Malaysian Chinese are no exception.

Beginning with little more than the clothes on their backs, the Chinese saved much of the money they earned as unskilled laborers. Years later, they had their own tiny businesses. Generations later, they were earning double the income of the Malays.

From a purely economic point of view, the productivity and thrift of the Chinese were to everyone's advantage. Malays retained much of their traditional way of life, while also enjoying some of the modern amenities made possible by the businesses, industries, and financial credit created by the Chinese. But politically, the situation became explosive.

The whole modern economic structure in Malaysia, created largely by the Chinese and by foreigners, is today seen politically as something "taken over" by them. It is almost as if whole industries came into existence by themselves—or "somehow"—and alien elements then grabbed control of them. Such is the magic of political rhetoric.

—November 20, 1984

VIII

POTPOURRI

Banning Boxing

Every tragedy that strikes a boxer brings forth renewed demands that the sport be banned. But, no matter how many people are killed or injured in mountain climbing, scuba diving, skiing, boating, or horseback riding, no one ever suggests that these activities be banned.

There are more than ten times as many fatalities in scuba diving alone as there are in boxing. There are more than a hundred times as many in boating.

The poor box. The affluent climb mountains, ride horses, go boating, skiing, or scuba diving. The affluent are regarded as adults with the right to make their own decisions and take their own risks. The poor are treated as wards, almost as the property, of humanitarians.

The tragic disease that recently struck Muhammad Ali has been blamed on boxing, even though it strikes many people who have never boxed. I am not a physician, so I don't know. Neither do most of the people who are pontificating that boxing should be banned.

The alternatives open to most people who become boxers are few and very poor. Only one heavyweight champion of the world has had a college degree—Gene Tunney, more than half a century ago. Many champions have had very little education or job skills. It is hard to see how they could have earned a decent living any other way—much less have a chance at some of the good things of life that are taken for granted by writers who denounce boxing.

The lives boxers led before they became boxers suggest how limited their options were. Some were delinquents or petty criminals. Jack Dempsey was once a hobo. Heavyweight champion James J. Braddock had been on welfare.

If people can become test pilots, stunt men, or lion tamers, in order to try to better their condition or make their mark in the world, then why deny the same opportunities—and risks—to those whose only hope is boxing?

The crusade against boxing is part of a general mindset that is very noble in its rhetoric and very ugly in its implications. There is nothing humanitarian about destroying one of the options of people who have very few options. This point is repeatedly forgotten or ignored in crusades for everything from slum clearance to so-called "consumer protection" laws.

These issues may seem remote from boxing, but the underlying principle is the same.

Slum clearance, for example, is essentially a matter of reducing the options of those with few options in order to please observers with many options. No one likes slums, including the people who live in them. Slum-dwellers are well aware that there is better housing available elsewhere—at a price.

While it is possible for many slum-dwellers to pay a higher price for housing, the sacrifices this would impose on their purchases of food, clothing, and other goods are not worth it to them. Otherwise, they would have made a different trade-off.

Crusaders who push for "slum clearance" by government are simply reducing the options of the poor, and forcing them into trade-offs that will please observers. Studies that show the former slum-dwellers living in better housing, after the slums have been torn down, miss the point completely. They could have moved into better housing before—if they were willing to make the sacrifices that have now been forced on them.

An increase in the housing supply would represent more options. But government policy over the years has consistently destroyed more housing than it has created. This has been especially true of low-income housing. Yet reducing the options of the poor through "slum clearance" is considered to be humanitarian. It is in fact the height of arrogance.

Many so-called "consumer protection" laws likewise represent arrogance masquerading as humanitarianism. All sorts of goods are sold in different quality levels, with correspondingly different prices. Different levels of product guarantees are also available, ranging from none at all at a flea market to money-back guarantees at more reputable—and more expensive—places.

In short, consumer protection costs money, like everything else. People already have the option of deciding how much consumer protection they want to pay for. What so-called "consumer protection" laws do is reduce the consumer's option. Crusaders decide how much protection is needed—and consumers are forced to pay for it, since businessmen are not about to absorb the inevitable cost increases. Once more, crusaders go away feeling noble, after making people worse off.

The repeated attempts to ban boxing are part of the same mindset. Boxing needs a lot better regulation. It does not need banning. The people who go into boxing need more and better options—beginning with a decent education, job skills, and work experience.

They do not need one of their few options taken away to please other people.

—October 25, 1984

The Case of the Fascinating Customer

It can happen in any business. But airlines seem especially prone to let it happen: One customer with a fascinating problem can tie up half a dozen employees, while lines of other customers look on helplessly.

Scene: Podunk International Airport in the busy season. Three long lines of travelers are waiting at an airline check-in counter. At the front of one line is a customer with a problem. It is a worst-case scenario: a pretty young woman in line and a man behind the counter.

She says, "I am flying to Paris but would like to make a stop in the Bahamas."

"Fine."

"And also in Chicago."

"O.K. Not exactly on the way but we can work something out. Let me see what the computer says."

"I'd like to charge the Chicago part of the trip on American Express and the trip to the Bahamas on MasterCard."

"No problem, ma'am. Any special reason?"

"Well, part of the trip is business and part is for pleasure, so I'm trying to separate the expenses."

"Good idea. Lots of people try to stick the company for everything. Now, how are you going to pay for the part of the trip from the Bahamas to Paris?"

"I already have a ticket from my travel agent for that."

"All right. And will you need a return ticket to Podunk— I hope?"

"Yes. And I want to pay for that with traveler's checks."

"Are they in dollars?"

"No, francs."

214

"I'm not quite sure how to handle that. Maybe Carol over here can tell me. Carol, do you have a minute?"

Carol is busy with a long line of her own customers, but she stops to help—and they wait.

"What's the problem, Bill?"

"Well, this lady is flying to France via Chicago and the Caribbean."

"Not a bad trick," Carol says.

"I can work that part out on the computer," Bill says. "But she wants to pay for part of the trip with traveler's checks in francs."

"That's O.K. unless she's taking the vacation special at 20 percent off."

The customer breaks in: "That is what I am taking!"

"Well, for that," Carol says, "I think you have to put everything on one credit card and stay a minimum of three weeks."

"I can't do that. I have to be back in time for a wedding."

"Yours?" Carol asks.

"No. I wish it was."

All three laugh. None of the people in line laughs.

"Maybe Shirley can figure something out," Carol suggests. "Shirley!"

Shirley is handling the third line. But she stops and comes over to huddle with Carol, Bill, and the customer.

Shirley is a breezy redhead. "Hi there," she says to the customer. "What can I do for you?"

Bill answers for her: "Well, this lady here," he says, looking at the name on the ticket. "Miss Marjorie Hartman—"

"Bill always likes to get the names of female customers," Shirley interjects, setting off another round of laughter—again confined to those at the counter.

"Anyway," Bill says, blushing slightly, "she wants to take the vacation special but can't stay three weeks and can't put it all on one credit card."

"Oh, listen," says Shirley, "I'll bet we can get an exception if we phone headquarters."

"You think so?" Bill says, beaming.

"Why not? It's worth a try," Shirley replies.

"Yeah," Carol adds as Shirley dials, "I'd like to find out myself."

"Service to the customer is our company's motto," Bill says proudly.

A surly customer in line mutters something about not getting any service, but it is drowned out in the hilarity at the counter.

"Hello, headquarters? Let me speak to the Vice President in charge of customer relations." After a pause, Shirley turns to the others gathered around her: "He's out of the office. Shall I phone the President of the company?"

"Yeah," Bill says. "Go for it!"

"Make him earn that big salary," Carol says.

"Hello. Put me through to the President. . . ."

—November 17, 1986

Nuns on Welfare

If we needed any further proof of the way values have been stood on their heads in these trendy times, we got it in a recent news story about aging nuns who have been forced to go on welfare. While the bishops' well-publicized pastoral letters have been morally condemning American society for lack of "compassion" (and everything else from economics to foreign policy), those same bishops have been letting elderly nuns be neglected, after years of dedicated service to the church and the society.

Whole generations of Catholic immigrants were educated and Americanized by nuns. Long before liberal intellectuals suddenly discovered that there were black people in America, nuns were helping to educate them as well. They still do. In ghettoes across the country, the nuns' low pay is what enables many parochial schools to continue offering a first-rate education for a few hundred dollars a year.

Not all aging nuns are being forced to stand in welfare lines with winos and pregnant teenagers. But well over a thousand nuns are estimated to be on public assistance. Some orders of nuns are staving off this eventuality by selling their property to make ends meet. But that is a stopgap measure which works only until they run out of convents and other buildings to sell.

Ironically, the same Archbishop R. G. Weakland who is the darling of the liberal media for his calls for more government giveaways—at home and abroad—has balked at funding a very modest retirement plan for nuns. There is money to feed bums at soup kitchens, money for a Washington staff to turn out politicized and sophomoric manifestoes for Weakland and his colleagues to publicize in the media, but the nuns can be left to fend for themselves.

Feeding those who refuse to work and neglecting nuns who have given a lifetime of service to others is symptomatic of a national problem of upside-down values. It is by no means peculiar to Catholics. On the contrary, many others went down this road sooner and further, and only in recent years have some of the bishops climbed on the bandwagon.

Liberal-left clergymen of various denominations often try to make what they say sound as if it came right out of the Bible. But Archbishop Weakland was honest enough to say that the famous (or notorious) pastoral letter on the American economy which his committee produced was based on thinking that comes from the secular "enlightenment" writers of the eighteenth century. In other words, it follows what the political left has been saying for 200 years.

The bishops are also following the classic pattern of the secular political left by loving mankind in the abstract, out on the horizon somewhere—and ignoring the suffering of flesh-and-blood human beings right in front of them. They again echo the secular left in not making moral distinctions between the deserving unfortunates and the undeserving hustlers spawned by indiscriminate handouts.

Any society that fails to distinguish between those who help build it up and those who tear it down has the moral equivalent of AIDS. Growing numbers of nuns relegated to welfare are a poignant symptom of this deeper social tragedy.

—May 27, 1986

Confessions of an Exploited Teenager

Many years ago, when I was a teenager, I worked at Jack's Grocery Store in Harlem, delivering groceries and doing little chores around the store.

One of my chores was to keep the cooler filled with beer and soda. This was one of those old-fashioned coolers—a sort of square vat where you sat the bottles and put in little chunks of ice. As the ice melted, you had a pool of cold water that chilled the drinks.

Before I first filled the cooler, Jack explained certain things. Although he wanted the cooler kept full, he warned me against trying to force too many bottles together. When you did that with a beer bottle, it could explode in your hand. (The glass was thin during World War II.)

"Do you understand?" he asked.

"Yes." (What did he think I was, a dummy?)

Before very long, I was busy filling up the cooler—and forcing bottles together. Suddenly there was a loud noise and I found myself holding the jagged neck of a beer bottle, while the beer and fragments of glass were spread all over the cooler.

It was a mess. We had to empty the whole cooler and drain it. And we couldn't leave pieces of broken glass in there for customers to cut their hands on. So all those little pieces had to be carefully picked out, one by one.

Jack seemed to take a couple of deep breaths before saying anything to me, as if he were trying to control himself. He seemed terribly irritable to me. Anybody could make a mistake.

Some days later, I was again filling up the cooler. Jack made some remark that I thought was sarcastic, so I just ignored it. Everything was going fine until the cooler was just about full. Then suddenly there was a loud noise. I found myself holding the top half of a beer bottle, while the bottom half was all over the cooler.

It was startling. Who would have thought something like that would happen? I was amazed. Jack seemed dumbfounded too.

I told Jack I was never going to do that again. But never isn't all that long when you are a teenager. Exploding beer bottles became a way of life at Jack's Grocery Store.

Each time it caught me completely by surprise. Some of the customers thought it was funny. Jack never did. He threatened to fire me.

I thought that was very harsh.

Decades later, I wondered how Jack found the patience to put up with me. If our roles had been reversed, I would probably have thrown him out on his ear.

Not all my employers were as patient as Jack. Only so often could you keep forgetting what they told you and still have a job. They even got mad when you came in late.

Losing a job was rough, especially after I left home and was on my own at seventeen. Back in those days, hunger was *my* problem—not the government's problem or Ed Meese's problem.

I still thought it was a pain to have to get up early and keep watching the clock, in order to get to work on time. But, as between punctuality and hunger, I quickly discovered that I preferred punctuality. In fact, I learned a lot of things much faster than I did at Jack's Grocery Store.

What is the moral of the story? That nobody should be a teenager? There is probably something to be said for that. But, since science has not yet found a cure for adolescence, the best we can do is give the only real antidote for immaturity—experience.

When I was a teenager, jobs were a lot easier to come by. Black teenage unemployment today is several times higher than it was then.

One of the reasons employers could afford to hire me was that my pay was very low—about what I was worth. The minimum wage law was not effective then. It wasn't changed for a dozen years after being enacted, so inflation had rendered it meaningless. Many low-wage industries were not even covered by the law.

Then came humanitarian politics, the politics of "compassion" as they now call it. No one could bear to see young people "exploited" by employers. The minimum wage was raised repeatedly and its coverage spread into almost every nook and cranny of the economy. You don't see exploited teenagers in the ghetto anymore. Instead, they are standing around on street corners, often getting into trouble. Humanitarians feel a lot better.

—October 7, 1984

Babe Ruth

This year is an anniversary of many historic events connected with the end of World War II. But it is also the 50th anniversary of the end of the career of the greatest baseball player who ever lived—Babe Ruth.

Some say that Ty Cobb was the greatest ball player. Others say Willie Mays. Many expected Mickey Mantle to reach that pinnacle, before injuries began plaguing his career. But Ruth was in a class by himself. His two great home-run records have been eclipsed but his overall performance remains unmatched.

They call someone an all-around player if he can hit and field, but no one except Babe Ruth was so all-around that he left pitching records as well as hitting records. No one else ever led the league in shutouts, victories, and lowest earned run average, as well as in home runs and batting average. No one else even came close to achieving all five distinctions in his career.

Babe Ruth began his career as a pitcher with the Boston Red Sox. Twice he won more than 20 games a season and one year he pitched nine shutouts—still the American League record for a lefthanded pitcher. In the next two years' World Series, he set another pitching record, with more than 29 consecutive scoreless innings. The latter record lasted longer than his 60 home-run record, and was in fact broken the same year.

The Red Sox were so desperate for hitters that they turned their star pitcher into a part-time outfielder. Playing fewer than 100 games altogether, Ruth led the league in home runs. From then on he was strictly a full-time slugger.

The Red Sox were in trouble financially as well as in hitting, so in 1920 they now tried another desperate gamble with Ruth. They sold him to the Yankees. This gamble blew up in their faces. The Red Sox never got into another World Series for 26 years. The Yankees, who had never been in a World Series, won seven pennants with Babe Ruth in the lineup. The only time they finished out of the first division was when Ruth was out sick in 1925.

Before he became fat in his later years, Ruth was also quite a base runner and covered a lot of ground in the outfield. Twice he stole 17 bases in a season, and over his career he stole home ten times—putting him ahead of Lou Brock in that department.

The greatness of Ruth, of course, centers on his hitting, and especially his slugging. To appreciate Ruth's greatness as a slugger, you have to realize how often he was not allowed to bat. He was walked more than any other man in the history of baseball—more than 2,000 times, which is like not being allowed to bat for more than three years. Ruth was walked 177 times in one season—more than once a game.

In proportion to his times at bat, no one ever hit home runs with the frequency of Babe Ruth, either in a season or over a lifetime. Roger Maris was walked fewer than 100 times the year he hit 61 home runs, because it was a bad gamble to walk Maris and pitch to Mickey Mantle, who had a much higher batting average. Hank Aaron had nearly 4,000 more official times at bat than Ruth—equivalent to about eight seasons. He was also never walked 100 times in a season.

Slugging averages tell more about a hitter than batting averages. Ruth's slugging average records, for a season or a lifetime, remain unchallenged by anyone. With batting averages, a single counts the same as a home run, but slugging averages are based on total bases. A slugging average of .700 means seven total bases every ten times at bat—three singles and a home run, for example—and has not been achieved by anyone in the past quarter of a century. Babe Ruth topped .700 nine times during his career, and his lifetime slugging average is only a few points lower.

To give some idea of Ruth's dominance as a slugger, such great sluggers as Hank Aaron, Joe DiMaggio, Willie Mays, and Hank Greenberg—in their best seasons—never reached the lifetime slugging average that Babe Ruth maintained over a 22-year period. He was in a class by himself.

—October 8, 1985

Tom Brokaw's "Patriotism"

"**I** know of no more patriotic group than television journalists."

That's what the man said.

He's Tom Brokaw, NBC News anchorman, featured in full-page ads recently. The ads are titled "Tom Brokaw Off Camera"—but have three big photos of him. You figure that out.

Figuring out how television journalists rated so high on patriotism is even tougher. When American soldiers went into Grenada a couple of years ago, the entire media made up its mind that we were wrong, before a single reporter set foot on the island.

The media and liberal politicians were denouncing President Reagan full blast, when the first rescued young Americans came home. When one of them knelt down and kissed American soil, the deep thinkers had the ground cut out from under them.

When the people of Grenada began expressing their gratitude for being rescued from the murderers who had seized the country, the media had to start backing off. When the other small nations in the region expressed their relief that a Communist military threat in their backyard was gone, there was really very little left for the media to say.

Another big surprise to the media was the widespread public support for the administration's decision to keep them out of Grenada until the military situation was under control. Many Americans saw the media as an undermining factor that our soldiers didn't need when they were under fire.

Maybe that is why this image-making advertising campaign has to claim "patriotism" for the TV news-readers. If a husband took out a full-page ad claiming that he was faithful to his wife, would we be reassured or suspicious?

Brokaw's claim of "patriotism" is followed by the assertion that "we're not mindless cheerleaders." We have to concede that they are not cheerleaders, though the jury is still out on "mindless."

Their biases are as predictable as elections in Russia.

Survey after survey among journalists themselves have shown their views to be overwhelmingly liberal-left. While the public has not read most of these surveys, they have reached the very same conclusion just from watching them. Part of the shock of the Grenada episode to the media was the discovery that ordinary Americans saw right through them.

Television journalists will go after a businessman or a president like he was a war criminal. But let Ralph Nader or Gloria Steinem come on, and they are treated like messiahs with a holy message for a troubled world.

The media don't just report news. They put white hats

and black hats on people, so that they come out looking like the good guys and the bad guys.

Brokaw's own image-advertisement betrays this mindset. He attacks "what big money can get done in Washington"—something we should all be concerned about. But when you watch television news, this is almost invariably an attack on the money spent by business lobbies or groups like the National Rifle Association.

Almost never is there a breath of criticism of the even bigger money spent by the Sierra Club or by liberal Common Cause. From where the media sit, these are the good guys.

The media journalists are also blissfully unconcerned about corruption of the democratic process by willful judges or by organized rioters whom the media insist on calling "demonstrators." If the rioters advocate disarmament, then they are "peace" activists. Either way they are the good guys.

Let the media discover that any of the sins that have plagued the human race for thousands of years still exist in the United States, and it becomes a special condemnation of American society. The morally anointed are constantly outraged that we have not obliterated racism, poverty, or disease. It would be fascinating to know who has—and how. But a look around the world shows that our problems in these areas are like a sprained ankle compared to cancer.

We ought to do something about the sprained ankle, but we shouldn't talk nonsense about it—much less call the nonsense "patriotism."

—March 22, 1985

Old-Timers

It made me feel like an old-timer when I heard that Mel Queen had become a baseball coach, after his pitching career was over. I saw his father pitch—as a rookie.

It made me feel like an old-timer when I asked a clerk in a record store about a famous record narrated by the great newscaster Edward R. Murrow—and she asked if he was rock or country-and-western.

Are you an old-timer?

You're an old-timer if you know what a fountain pen, a Speed Graphic, or an automobile crank was.

You're an old-timer if the name "Sugar Ray" makes you think of Robinson instead of Leonard.

You're definitely mature if you can remember when Ronald Reagan was a member of Americans for Democratic Action.

You're an old-timer if you can recall when the word "gay" connoted a lively interest in the opposite sex.

You're eligible for a Senior Citizen discount if you can remember the last time the federal government balanced the budget.

You're no yuppie if you can recall when school children were afraid of the teacher, instead of vice versa.

If you saw Roger Maris the year he broke Babe Ruth's home-run record, that was a quarter of a century ago, old-timer.

You're an old-timer if you can remember when a woman's bathing suit contained more material than a man's scarf.

You're an old-timer if you can remember when sportsmen were expected to show sportsmanship.

If you can remember when taxi drivers in New York were civil, then there are a lot of miles on your speedometer.

If you can remember when people who refused to work were called "bums" instead of "the homeless," then you are from a different era.

You're an old-timer if you can remember when you were more likely to hear four-letter words in a bar than in a movie.

You've been around for a while if you can remember when civil rights organizations said that race should not be taken into account in hiring decisions.

If you can remember when you could always tell boys from girls at a glance, then you are a golden oldie.

If you don't end your sentences with prepositions, or use "you know" as a comma, then you are not keeping up with the times.

If you can remember when the leading basketball stars were Jewish, then you should take the elevator instead of walking up the stairs.

If you can instantly identify "the king of swing," "the brown bomber," and "the little flower," then you shouldn't have to produce I.D. when you order a drink.

If New Year's eve makes you think of Guy Lombardo and Ben Grauer, then you're not part of the Pepsi generation but the Geritol set.

You're an old-timer if the name "Rocky" makes you think of Graziano or Marciano instead of Sylvester Stallone.

You're an old-timer if you can remember when people didn't talk so much about moral issues—and didn't require so many devices to prevent shop-lifting.

You're an old-timer if you can close your eyes and visualize the silhouette of a P-38—or of Betty Grable.

If you can remember when the post office wasn't as modern but the mail travelled faster, then you're an old-timer.

If you saw the St. Louis Browns play baseball, then you shouldn't be flirting with young waitresses—and if you saw them win their only pennant, you shouldn't even be thinking about such things.

Don't even call yourself middle-aged if you can remember when people didn't lock their doors.

You're an old-timer if you can remember when emaciated women were more likely to be poor than to be models.

If you can remember every one of these things, then you have a good shot at some longevity records.

—May 8, 1986

By the Numbers

When intellectuals discover that the world does not behave according to their theories, the conclusion they invariably draw is that the world must be changed. It must be awfully hard to change theories.

The prevailing unproven dogma of the intellectuals today is that groups would be evenly distributed statistically, if it were not for arbitrary barriers, discrimination and other forms of social malaise.

Courts of law listen solemnly while statistics are used to show that the ethnic, sex, or other balance of some company's employees could not be the result of random chance. Once that is shown, the company is well on its way to being convicted of discrimination, even if it applied the same hiring and promotion standards to everybody.

Applying statistical analysis of random events would make sense if human beings were random events. But groups differ around the world, and they have differed throughout history. In the simple task of collecting sap from rubber trees in colonial Malaya, the average Chinese worker produced twice the output of the average Malay worker. In India's state of Andra Pradesh, farmers from the coastal region have gotten three times the output per acre of farmers from the interior—even when the coastal farmers moved into the interior and farmed the same land just used by interior farmers.

In baseball, there were seven consecutive years in which no white man won the National League's Most Valuable Player Award. Given the racial make-up of the United States, the odds against that happening by random chance are more than 600,000 to 1. But the fact that it wasn't pure chance does not mean that there was collusion or discrimination against whites.

Far from behaving randomly, groups show the most pronounced patterns, persisting for centuries in very different societies. The military achievements of Germans have not been confined to Germany, but go back thousands of years in other countries as well. More than once, the entire army of the Roman Empire was headed by a general of German ancestry—and the same has been true in czarist Russia, and in the United States in both world wars. Germans in czarist Russia were 1 percent of the population and 40 percent of the military officers.

People do not immigrate randomly. During the great era of Italian immigration to the Western Hemisphere, most people from southern Italy went to North America, while most people from northern Italy went to South America. Figure that out. People from towns just a few miles apart in Italy settled on opposite coasts of Australia. Similar patterns are common in other countries: Most prewar Japanese immigrants from around Hiroshima went to the United States, those from Nagasaki to China, and those from Okinawa to the Philippines. In the Balkans, more than half the population of one Macedonian village immigrated to Toronto.

People who go on to higher education from different

social or ethnic backgrounds do not specialize in the same mix of subjects. The Japanese and the Hispanics specialize in a drastically different mix of subjects, whether you compare Japan with Hispanic countries or Japanese Americans with Hispanic Americans. In India, untouchables who attend the universities do not choose the same subjects as other castes. Nor do the Central Asians in the Soviet Union choose a random mix of subjects, or the same mix as other ethnic groups. Nor do all groups perform at the same level. More than half the students in Sri Lanka who received an A on the university mathematics entrance examination were from the small (and oppressed) Tamil minority. Similar results can be found for Chinese, Japanese, or Jewish students in the United States and other countries.

These many peoples have undoubtedly all had their reasons for their decisions, and there were undoubtedly also reasons why performance levels in the same activities have differed so dramatically—whether or not observers will ever know what all these reasons were. But reason is not randomness. It is time to tell the intellectuals that their theories are wrong—and that we are not going to tear the world apart trying to make reality conform to their preconceptions. It would make a good New Year's resolution.

—December 10, 1985

An "Epidemic" of Irresponsibility

There seem to be more epidemics sweeping across this country now than in the ages of the great plagues. A recent cover story in *Newsweek* magazine referred to an "epidemic" of drug use among young people. Before that, the media were sounding the alarm about "epidemics" of teenage pregnancy, of alcoholism, and of suicides, among many other things.

When I was growing up, we were taught to stay away from crowded places during an epidemic, because someone might sneeze on you and you would come down with influenza or something. It is hard to see how you are going to come down with drug addiction—much less pregnancy—that way.

Reckless use of the word "epidemic" is more than just media hype debasing the language. Like most clever uses of words, it camouflages a hidden agenda. Personal responsibility is anathema to deep thinkers, for that would undermine their role as rescuers of the "victims" of society.

If everything is an "epidemic," then we have done an end run around personal responsibility and can now break into the clear with more government programs—which means more money, power, and visibility for the rescuers. It is an old script, but the anointed keep using it, changing a few words here and there to keep on bamboozling the public.

Personal responsibility can be gotten rid of in many ways. Comedian Flip Wilson says, "The devil made me do it." Deep thinkers say "society" made people do it. That means the taxpayers have to pick up the tab. Flip Wilson is much funnier, and not nearly as costly.

There are people with some unusual names. Just among economists, there are Orley Ashenfelter, Axel Leijonhufvud ("pronounced just the way it's spelled," he says) and Pedro Schwartz. But I have never met anybody named "society." Yet, if you believe the deep thinkers, this is who is making everybody do everything.

Everyone is learning how to cop out of personal responsibility by blaming "society." From teenagers in high school to hardened felons in prison, they can tell you how the "traumas" they were put through by "society" caused everything from failing grades to armed robbery. People who would rather mooch than work used to be called bums, but now they are homeless "victims" of "society." You are supposed to feel guilty because more money is not being taken out of your paycheck to support them in the manner to which they would like to become accustomed.

The decline of personal responsibility has been accompanied by a rise in social responsibility by people who had nothing to do with the individual decisions that brought on disaster. Along with this has come an increased role for people skilled at creating guilt.

One of the best performances of this nature was a television appearance years ago by author James Baldwin. He glared out from the TV screen in a coldly bitter stare, saying: "I've just come from seeing a dead boy—and you killed him."

"Not me, Jim," I replied to the screen, "I've been here in the apartment all day."

It turned out that this "dead boy" was 28 years old and had died from an overdose of drugs. Baldwin never really explained how the television viewers had done him in— nor did he have to. "Society" is presumed guilty until proven innocent.

We laugh at people who believe in the tooth fairy, but we take it seriously when deep thinkers talk about "society" as having done this or that—or having failed to do this or that. If they mean the government, then they ought to say the government. But then we might see through the high-toned words to the hidden agenda.

—March 17, 1986

New Year's Resolutions

Most New Year's resolutions are going to be broken. But they can still serve a purpose, by reminding us of where we need to think about improving.

In that spirit, here are some New Year's resolutions for the government.

The first order of business is the deficit. One of the reasons it is so out of control is that no individual Congressman is held responsible for contributing to it.

The government's New Year's resolutions should include some method of calculating a deficit for each Congressman. All the appropriations he voted for should be added up. All the taxes he voted for should also be added up.

If he played the usual game of being in favor of spending and against taxing, then the size of his personal deficit should be published—preferably just before he is up for re-election.

Another New Year's resolution should be to organize a corps of civilians, who will operate as police auxiliaries in high-crime neighborhoods, one weekend per month.

No one should be allowed to be appointed as a judge until after serving three years in these police auxiliaries in high-crime neighborhoods.

But police auxiliaries should not be limited to judges. A special effort should also be made to recruit members of the American Civil Liberties Union and editorial writers for the liberal news media.

Many of these people would probably not live to finish their three-year terms—especially if they tried to practice the philosophy they preach in the safety of the court room or in editorial offices.

But their first-hand experience might enable them to solve a problem that always seems to fascinate them: How to capture armed and dangerous people, without hurting the little darlings. They might discover a simple fact—that increasing the safety of criminals is easy, if you are willing to jeopardize policemen.

It has been said that the number of dead policemen is of no interest to liberals. Now it would be.

A third New Year's resolution should be to apply television's "fairness" doctrine to nature programs. Under the fairness doctrine, broadcasters are supposed to present both sides of political issues.

It is also called the "equal time" principle. And it is carried to great lengths.

Back in 1980, a local television station happened to broadcast an old Ronald Reagan movie during the primary election campaign. The government made them give equal time to all the other candidates.

No such principle applies to television nature programs. Yet these programs provide the most one-sided political propaganda on the air. It is virtually impossible to watch a single nature program without getting political lobbying for the kind of environmental policies favored by the Sierra Club. They contain no hint that there is any other possible point of view.

Application of the fairness doctrine would mean that the viewing public would finally be told that there are costs to letting herds of elephants run loose, trampling crops, in countries where there is barely enough food to keep people alive.

Even in affluent America, there are costs to environmentalist obstruction of the building of hydroelectric dams, oil drilling, or nuclear power plants. While nature program hosts wail over the lost nesting sites of birds or the lost spawning grounds of salmon, thousands of men go down into coal mines to get the energy denied us in other ways. And, every year, many of those coal miners never come back alive. Let the nature programs show that—alongside their pictures of oil on the feathers of pelicans.

Or let them get out of politics entirely and talk about nature.

Finally, the government's New Year's resolutions should include a plan to give every newborn baby a gold-embossed certificate of moral superiority. That would do away with the need for moral posturing behind so many damn fool policies that are advocated.

—December 27, 1984

The Fourth of July

No holiday so separates most Americans from the deep-thinking elite as the Fourth of July. Most of us know that, whatever our color or condition, and wherever we came from, we are better off here.

We need only see the hunger in Africa, the blood in

Lebanon, or the Berlin wall to realize how lucky we are. Even among free nations, America is blessed.

Deep thinkers don't look at it that way. The very phrase "Fourth of July" can bring scorn to their faces. Anything "the masses" believe in is suspect in their eyes. They don't compare the United States to other countries but to their ideals. Every wrong in this country—past or present—proves to them that it is not worthy of noble creatures like themselves.

It never occurs to them that tragic wrongs are found wherever human beings are found. Anyone looking for a sinner need look no further than the mirror. Everything human is a failure compared to ideals.

To build a beautiful world of ideals takes only an active imagination, some free time, and a nice vocabulary. But the world people live in is the world of reality. And to make that world decent and free takes much hard work, much sacrifice, and many young men buried under a sea of crosses at places like Normandy and Iwo Jima.

Ideals have their value, but ultimately ideal visions are a cheap substitute for reality. For those with the cheap substitute to look down their noses at the real thing is a little much.

If America could be summed up in one word, that word would be freedom. Those of us who grew up with freedom may take it for granted but tens of thousands have died trying to get here for it. In just one year, 40,000 people died trying to cross the Atlantic from Ireland alone, back in the days of the sailing ships. Even larger numbers of "boat people" have perished in the Pacific in our own time.

The desire for freedom is so much a part of human nature that politicians and deep thinkers try to call other things "freedom" in order to sell them. They try to call it "economic freedom" when the government guarantees you food, shelter, and other basics. Prisons have that kind of "freedom." So do Communist countries. People try to escape from both, often at the risk of their lives.

The freedom of America is the freedom to live your own life and take your own chances. The American Revolution was more than a rebellion against England. It was a rebellion against the whole idea that some special anointed could tell everybody else what to do. The Constitution of the United States is pervaded by the conviction that no one is to be trusted with too much power.

Long after kings and dukes have faded into the background, other kinds of the anointed have arisen, convinced that they should be running our lives for us. All sorts of beautiful things are supposed to happen if only we give enough power and money to the new anointed. If only we surrender our freedom to our betters, they will "solve" our "problems," and create "social justice." Haven't we heard that one before—too many times? Hasn't it been tried already in too many places, from Nazi Germany to Jonestown?

Freedom has to be defended every day, against lofty rhetoric as well as military threats. We have to say to the anointed: Look, you fellows may have your diplomas and high-toned talk, your good intentions and tables of statistics. You may even have some good ideas and suggestions now and then—and we will follow some of them, if we feel like it. But we're not going to let you run our lives. Hey, Mac—we're as good as you are. That's what America is all about.

—July 1, 1986

Twentieth Century Limited

As we approach the end of the year, we are also conscious of approaching the end of this century. People are already beginning to talk about the twenty-first century. But we ought to look where we have been before we imagine where we are going.

No century could have dawned with more hope than the twentieth century. Science and technology had brought undreamed-of progress to the lives of millions of human beings. Whether in agriculture or industry, output was growing by leaps and bounds. Mass killer diseases like smallpox were being defeated by medical science. The last great war to ravage the whole continent of Europe ended 85 years earlier, at Waterloo—and such horrors were considered permanently behind us.

Advances in the relationships among peoples showed similar signs of progress. Slavery, which had lasted for thousands of years on all continents, was wiped out throughout Western civilization, in a matter of decades. Jews, who had been locked up in ghettoes for centuries, now had equal rights in a large and growing number of nations, and held public office in England, the United States—and Germany.

The high hopes and expectations with which the twentieth century began gave no inkling that this would be the century in which we would have to coin such new expressions as "fascist," "world war," "genocide," and "thermonuclear." What went wrong?

Many things went wrong, of course, and historians will be kept busy for a long time trying to piece it all together. But, running through the complexities and agonies of this

238

century are two dominant forces: arrogance and propaganda.

The great achievements in science and technology, which transformed the face of the earth, led many to believe that they could politically transform the world, with equally beneficial results. In Russia, the son of a czarist official was planning a freer and better society, based on "scientific" social principles. He called himself Lenin. America began the twentieth century talking of its "manifest destiny" to be fulfilled by acquiring an empire, including the Philippines, Hawaii, and Puerto Rico. Germany began the century looking for its rightful "place in the sun," reflecting its sudden rise to industrial, scientific, and economic eminence. In the Orient, an isolated and backward nation called Japan had suddenly modernized and was ready to enter the world stage as a major power.

The romantic notion that hunger and poverty drive nations to war has been thoroughly discredited by the history of the twentieth century. The poor and the hungry have all they can do to survive. It is those who are full of themselves, who are starving for glory rather than food, who devastate whole continents and squander the blood and treasure of the human race—all for a few moments of strutting in a fading sun.

The three Axis nations whose aggressions produced World War II were all nations that either did not exist a hundred years earlier or whose existence no one knew or cared about. Italy became a nation in 1861 and Germany in 1871. Japan was a nation much longer but one living in utter isolation until the American navy forced their way in, in 1854, and opened it up to the world.

These were nations that had something to prove. And 40 million people died while they were trying to prove it.

The arrogance of conquerors has been proverbial, but the Japanese and Germans reached new highs—or lows. The Japanese conquerors were notorious for walking up

to men on the street and slapping their faces for no reason. The raping of nuns in Nanking, the sadistic murders
of the Bataan Death March, the wholesale slaughters of
civilians in Singapore, were all part of a Japanese pattern
in Asia that paralleled what the Nazis did in Europe. It was
the classic behavior of bullies trying to prove something.

So was the Holocaust, against people whose achievements and learning had to be galling to the kinds of "losers" who made up the Nazi movement. The previous
genocide in the First World War, against Armenians in
Turkey, was completely parallel as an attack on a more
successful and better educated minority by people with
every reason to envy them—and to feel inferior to them.
So was the mass slaughter of the Ibos in Nigeria and the
horrors inflicted on the "boat people" in Southeast Asia.

Propaganda is the other great factor that has played a
major role in the tragic history of the twentieth century.
Mass communications have given unprecedented leverage
to lies. Hitler was perhaps the ultimate master of this
twentieth-century phenomenon. But the Communists have
been a close second, and they were there before Hitler, as
well as after him.

The key feature of Communist propaganda has been
the depiction of people who are more productive as mere
exploiters of others. Sheer repetition has driven this doctrine deep into the consciousness of the world's intellectuals, whether Communist or non-Communist. It has spread
across the philosophic spectrum, even to the religious
community, where it is called "liberation theology." Facts
mean nothing to those who have been seized by this vision.

As we head toward the twenty-first century, we have
once again the central ingredients of the twentieth
century's tragedies. There is the arrogance of those who,
like Lenin, have the blueprint for Utopia in their pockets
and need only to gain the political levers of power to put
it into effect. There is the newly arrived great power, the

Soviet Union, and the enormous power of propaganda, dominated by the sanctified envy that justifies revenge against those better off—whether classes, races, or nations.

Add to this two new dimensions. One is a well-cultivated guilt in Western democracies that makes us hesitant and indecisive in the face of demagogic denunciations, outrageous demands, or even international terrorism. The other great factor is the nuclear threat. Given the technological superiority of the West, we can always make it suicidal for anyone to launch a nuclear attack—if we have the will to keep any potential aggressor from getting ahead of us. The psychic state of the Western world is, however, the great question as we move toward the twenty-first century.

—December 10, 1985

INDEX

243